HOPE IN TIMES OF CRISIS

The authors of this book are passionate about the vital connection between mission and ecumenism. The breadth of the book reveals the breadth of the connection between commitment to church unity and the commitment of Christians' participation in God's mission. In a fractured and fragile world, the churches have a crucial part to play in reconciliation and healing, and they will do it best if they do it together. With unity the Christian churches will have a chance of a prophetic presence in our contemporary complex world.

—Stephen Bevans, SVD Professor of Mission and Culture, Emeritus, Catholic Theological Union, Chicago

The authors confront the daunting challenge of reimagining Christian ecumenical mission in today's highly globalized, intertwined but rapidly fragmenting world that is fraught with geopolitical conflicts and suffering from a developmentalism that neglects God's Creation, thrives on inequality and ignores institutionalized injustices. Providing snapshots of the checkered history of mission in the ecumenical movement using post-colonial and post-modern lenses, the work critically highlights many of the questionable biases and perspectives embedded in traditional approaches to mission.

—Theresa C. Carino, Consultant to the Amity Foundation, Nanjing, China

Hope in Times of Crisis is a bold and prophetic call for renewal and reimagining of ecumenical mission in the context of heightened challenges in the new century. The book charts a delicate new relationship between mission and Christian unity with balance, tension, and complementarity while urging Christ's church to present the genuine message of hope to the suffering world—a critical proposition to renew mission thinking and practice.

—Wonsuk Ma, Distinguished Professor of Global Christianity, Oral Roberts University

There is a spirit of serious criticism of mission in the past and a desire to integrate missionary efforts into fighting the threats to the environment and humanity. This offers hope that the gospel will be better transmitted to today's troubled societies and, above all, to every image of God seeking a way out of the tragic dead ends of the present temporary life.

—Dimitra Koukoura, Professor of Homiletics, Emerita, Aristotle University of Thessaloniki

Contemporary, comprehensive and compelling . . . A must-read for scholars and practitioners of world mission and ecumenism. This book takes us forward. The distinct contribution that this volume offers is a contextual global perspective on the convergence of mission and unity and its implications for today's crises-ridden world.

>—Metropolitan Dr. Geevarghese Mor Coorilos,
> former Moderator, WCC Commission on World Mission and Evangelism (CWME)

This visionary book explores contemporary global crises, and shows how ecumenical mission—past, present, and future—provides hope for abundant life. Featuring a dialogical and collaborative approach, leading ecumenists show that covenanted community and spiritual discernment can be world changing. In the age of world Christianity, collaborative and networked mission encourages resilience by deepening the relationship among God, humanity, and the created world. I highly recommend this book as an exceptionally thoughtful application of the ecumenical mission tradition to the complex realities facing God's people today.

>—Dana L. Robert, William Fairfield Warren Distinguished Professor,
> Boston University

This book is indeed a product of long and intensive discernment by the people who are best placed to do that. It is set in the context of contemporary world and its challenges, in their intersectionality. While it is honest about the challenges, it is really providing hope, unlike the many melancholic, defeatist approaches which only demonize mission. The concept of mission is upheld, asking how we can responsibly continue to address our challenges while taking advantage of learnings from the past mistakes.

>—Fidon R. Mwombeki, General Secretary,
> All Africa Conference of Churches

The book proposes a holistic and trinitarian model for mission, one that respects diversity while advocating for unity, and sees convergence in evangelization and diaconia as a genuine expression of faith; as witness to God's love for humankind, expressed in His incarnation and resurrection. Mission has a transformative character, and we are part of *Missio Dei*. As an Orthodox Christian, I enthusiastically welcome this effort, offering hope in times of ambivalence and turbulence, and viewing mission as a life-affirming expression of faith in modern times.

>—Evi Voulgaraki-Pissina, Senior Lecturer in Missiology,
> National and Kapodistrian University of Athens

Hope in Times of Crisis

Reimagining Ecumenical Mission

∽

MARINA NGURSANGZELI BEHERA
MICHAEL BIEHL
RISTO JUKKO
KENNETH R. ROSS

Forewords by Esther Mombo and
Raimundo Barreto Jr.

CASCADE *Books* · Eugene, Oregon

HOPE IN TIMES OF CRISIS
Reimagining Ecumenical Mission

Copyright © 2025 Wipf and Stock Publishers. All rights reserved. Except for brief quotations in critical publications or reviews, no part of this book may be reproduced in any manner without prior written permission from the publisher. Write: Permissions, Wipf and Stock Publishers, 199 W. 8th Ave., Suite 3, Eugene, OR 97401.

Cascade Books
An Imprint of Wipf and Stock Publishers
199 W. 8th Ave., Suite 3
Eugene, OR 97401

www.wipfandstock.com

PAPERBACK ISBN: 979-8-3852-2558-3
HARDCOVER ISBN: 979-8-3852-2559-0
EBOOK ISBN: 979-8-3852-2560-6

Cataloguing-in-Publication data:

Names: Behera, Marina Ngursangzeli, author. | Biehl, Michael, 1956–, author. | Jukko, Risto, author. | Ross, Kenneth R., author. | Mombo, Esther, foreword. | Barreto, Raimundo, foreword.

Title: Hope in times of crisis : reimagining ecumenical mission / Marina Ngursangzeli Behera, Michael Biehl, Risto Jukko, and Kenneth R. Ross ; forewords by Esther Mombo and Raimundo Barreto Jr.

Description: Eugene, OR : Cascade Books, 2025 | Includes bibliographical references.

Identifiers: ISBN 979-8-3852-2558-3 (paperback) | ISBN 979-8-3852-2559-0 (hardcover) | ISBN 979-8-3852-2560-6 (ebook)

Subjects: LCSH: Missions and Christian union. | Missions—Theory. | Christian Theology. | Ecumenical Studies.

Classification: BV2063 .B40 2025 (print) | BV2063 .B40 (ebook)

All Scripture quotations, unless otherwise indicated, are taken from the Holy Bible, New International Version®, NIV®. Copyright © 1973, 1978, 1984, 2011 by Biblica, Inc.™ Used by permission of Zondervan. All rights reserved worldwide. www.zondervan.com The "NIV" and "New International Version" are trademarks registered in the United States Patent and Trademark Office by Biblica, Inc.™

Where otherwise indicated, scripture quotations are taken from The Authorized (King James) Version. Rights in the Authorized Version in the United Kingdom are vested in the Crown. Reproduced by permission of the Crown's patentee, Cambridge University Press.

Table of Contents

Foreword by Esther Mombo xi
Foreword by Raimundo Barreto Jr. xv
Preface xix

CHAPTER 1: A World in Crisis 1
    Climate Crisis 4
    A World at War? 6
    Polarized Societies 7
    Inequality 8
    Bankrupt Politics 10
    The Human Person 11
    Mission a Matter of the Spirit 13
    Renewal of Ecumenical Vision 14
    Future and Hope 16

CHAPTER 2: The Earth We Need to Cherish 19
    The Crisis 21
    The Rethink 23
    Not Just One Monster, but Two 26
    Ecumenical Vision Inspiring Action 28

CHAPTER 3: The Economy We Need to Create 31
    Failure of the Economy 33
    Failure of Politics 36
    Building Alternative Vision 38
    Tending the Wounds 40

CHAPTER 4: The Development We Need to Empower 43
    Mission and Service 44

Table of Contents

Development Discourses 46
Mission Discourse 48
Development and Evangelism 52

CHAPTER 5: The People We Need to Become 55
On a Spiritual Wavelength 59
Transforming Disciples 61
Time to Move Together 64

CHAPTER 6: The Migration We Need to Welcome 67
"Birth Lottery" and the Web of Movement 68
Mission from the Margins 70
Bringing Back the Gospel 73
Reverse Mission? 75
Crossing Invisible Frontiers 76

CHAPTER 7: The Missionaries We Need to Envisage 78
Mission and Missionaries 81
Mission Everywhere 84
Mission in *Together Towards Life* 85
Being a Missionary and Being Missionary 87
And the Missionary Vocation? 90

CHAPTER 8: The Formation We Need to Offer 91
Education in Mission 92
Theological Education in the Ecumenical Movement 94
What We Need 96
  Missional Formation and Discipleship 98
  Education in a Contextual and Global Perspective 100
  Decolonization of Theology 101
  Digital / Online Education 102
A Way Forward 103

CHAPTER 9: The Complacency We Need to Explode 105
Unity and Fragmentation 106
Practicing Christian Division 107
Navigating Ecumenism 111
Mission as a Vantage Point 112
In Way of a Conclusion 115

TABLE OF CONTENTS

CHAPTER 10: The Triune God We Need to Adore in Unity 118
    Unity and Mission in the Trinity 121
    Ecumenical and Evangelical 125
    Unity and Ecumenical and Evangelical Mission 128
    Reconciled in Unity 132

CHAPTER 11: The Hope We Need to Imagine 133
    Learning from Ecumenical Experience 137
    Ecumenical Mission Means Hope 140
    Framework for Mission: Hope-Based Action 143
        Creation Awareness 147
        Eschatological Orientation 147
        Personal Transformation 147
        Humility and Reliance on God 148
        Holistic Engagement 148
        Prophetic Witness 148
        Solidarity and Hospitality 148
    Unity as Catholicity of the Church 149

Authors 151
Bibliography 153

Foreword

This book explains in a compelling way the multiplicity and diversity of how mission happens today, both in local contexts and in global relationality. As the authors rightly point out, mission is no longer solely about a flow of professional missionaries moving from one place to another. Rather, it is already happening everywhere, as the gospel takes root and bears fruit in myriad cultural and geographical settings. Therefore, the book invites readers to consider mission not merely as a journey from one place to another but as a dynamic, omnipresent force shaping communities both locally and globally.

As I am most familiar with the situation in Kenya, I will use it to reflect through it on the content the book. I would like to emphasize the importance of ecumenical mission in Kenya and how the complex history of ecumenical engagement can enrich the study and practice of mission. Along with colleagues from Eastern Africa I joined the international study process to celebrate the centenary of the founding of the International Missionary Council 1921–2021, one of the many times I collaborated with the authors of this book. The study process was a significant opportunity to show how the Kenyan church has been working to integrate the Christian faith into local cultures and worldviews. This process has faced challenges due to power dynamics and colonial legacies. However, it has led to a rich tapestry of ecumenical relations and theological reflection, influencing the trajectory of mission.

Ecumenical mission, with its history and programs, advocates for the visible unity of Christian denominations and the collaborative effort of churches worldwide. This is evident in Kenya, where diverse Christian traditions have united to address social, economic, political, and spiritual challenges. Ecumenical mission in Kenya shows how local contexts can influence and enhance global mission strategies, demonstrating that mission is an ongoing interaction between local and global perspectives.

Foreword

In our interconnected world, understanding mission as a global phenomenon is crucial. This book argues that mission must resonate deeply with the experiences of people at the grassroots level. Global crises such as environmental, economic, and social challenges demand a unified response that transcends geographical and cultural boundaries, and the book offers a vision for addressing these issues collectively.

Despite political, economic, and social upheavals, the church in Kenya has remained a beacon of hope for the nation. In times of crisis, the ecumenical movement has been at the forefront, mobilizing resources, advocating for justice, and providing pastoral care to communities in need. This crisis-driven nature of mission is a global theme, as the church responds to pandemics, natural disasters, and sociopolitical unrest worldwide. The book highlights how the ecumenical movement can offer vision and guidance in times of crisis, providing answers and hope amid adversity.

This book emphasizes the growing importance of local congregations in mission work. Traditionally, mission work was mainly seen as the responsibility of cross-cultural missionaries sent from one part of the world to another. However, today there is a shift in perspective. It is now widely recognized that local congregations are at the forefront of mission work, with a deep understanding of their own cultural and social contexts. This shift is particularly evident in Kenya, where local churches are taking the lead in mission initiatives, addressing the needs of their communities in culturally relevant and sustainable ways. This redefines the role of cross-cultural missionaries, emphasizing the importance of empowering local congregations and reducing dependence on external missionaries.

Looking back at the past century of ecumenical mission history, especially since the formation of the International Missionary Council in 1921, we can see a pattern of mission work being carried out during times of crisis. Whether it was during wartime, economic hardships, or social upheavals, mission work has always adapted to meet the needs of the moment. This history provides priceless insights into how mission work can address our contemporary crises.

One of the main themes that emerges from this history is the theme of hope. Even in the face of overwhelming challenges, ecumenical mission work consistently offers hope to distressed communities. This hope is not passive but instead involves active engagement in transforming societies. The stories of mission work in Kenya and other parts of the world illustrate how hope has been a driving force, inspiring individuals and communities to work towards a better future.

The final chapter of the book argues that by learning from the past, we can find innovative and effective ways to address today's crises. The history of ecumenical mission shows that mission work is not only about addressing immediate needs but also about nurturing long-term change and transformation. The focus on a global perspective, the priority of local congregations, and the lessons from history all point to a vision of mission work that is dynamic, inclusive, and hopeful. As we navigate the challenges of the twenty-first century, the legacy of ecumenical mission work offers us a road map for finding solutions and fostering unity. It reminds us that mission work is happening everywhere, in every context, and that by working together, we can create a more just and compassionate world.

Professor Esther Mombo, St. Paul's University, Limuru, Kenya

Foreword

The question of whether mission is redeemable has been a topic of discussion within the ecumenical movement since the 1960s. This book revisits the issue and suggests that examining the history of missions from an ecumenical perspective can, in fact, offer hope for the future amidst the global crises we face today.

In today's globalized reality, where, for instance, a war in Europe (the Russian invasion of Ukraine) has impacted the ability of families in North Africa and other parts of the world to eat bread, and international cooperation is urgently needed, the authors of this volume look to the churches and their ecumenical experiment with mission as a critical resource for civil society international mobilization. They propose that a reimagined ecumenical approach to mission can provide a vision for living together in a highly complex and deeply interconnected world. This missiological approach to addressing the global crisis demands a renewed understanding of creation and salvation that ties together the future of humanity and the whole of creation, especially in light of the challenges posed by climate change and a globalized neoliberal economy.

Drawing on the ecumenical understanding of *Missio Dei* and the need to build relations and trust between people of different faiths, the authors advance a theology of mission centered on the Spirit. Their approach to "reimagining the ecumenical vision" involves a radical shift in focus, from conversion to collaboration, from exclusivity to inclusivity. They aim at renewing, revamping, and reimagining the ecumenical vision. Thus, for them, mission is not only about the past but also about the present and the future. They propose a reckoning with the missionary past, including modern Christian complicity with the status quo, and the re-engagement with the international solidarity and collaborative spirit that has also characterized the mission movement, which can retrieve new forms of unity and discernment of God's purpose.

Foreword

While mission has often been associated with intolerance and exclusivism, the authors reclaim the term, making common cause with those resisting the forces of death and embracing everyday life. Their perspective on mission focuses on solidarity, justice, and love. This renewed look at the history of mission encourages learning from its errors and successes and offers a vision of hope and renewal.

More than a recipe, a theory, or a manual, this book, written by authors connected to different continents who see the impact of this multifaceted crisis from a varied perspective, is filled with the sensibility of those who, in the words of the late Brazilian archbishop Helder Camara, keep their ear on the ground. It calls for an urgent change of attitude, a change that must go beyond lip service to make the necessary impact. This widely ecumenical perspective engages the reader from various viewpoints and experiences. Their dedication to unity and cooperation, as shown in their ecumenical journey, is inspiring and invites readers to consider a similar approach in their own circumstances.

The interconnectedness of the environmental crisis and the profound economic inequality that divides our world, along with the inadequacy of current measures and discussions to make a significant change of course, lead these authors to delve into the deeper spiritual resources of our traditions in order to develop a revitalized ecumenical vision that can inspire unified transformative action.

The book is explicit that the challenges humanity faces today necessitate the development of a broad, inclusive movement that must involve the impoverished and the marginalized, or, as the authors put it, an ecumenism maximized to the highest degree. They caution that what is at stake is the planet itself. The ecumenical vision they propose is ambitious. It envisions a new economy, financial structure, a new brand of politics, and a new way of existing, thinking, and living in the world. This vision is not merely a theoretical concept, but serves a practical guide to equip readers with the necessary tools to effect change.

The vision advanced by the authors is not entirely new. However, this book issues a renewed appeal to various prophetic traditions. The authors position themselves with vulnerability, expressing their disappointments, raising critical queries, and listening to those they engage with on a daily basis, particularly the most vulnerable, i.e., those most directly impacted by the crises the book aims to address. In the ecumenical vision the book presents, Christians and churches from the Global South have a significant role.

Foreword

The amalgamation of the authors' diverse locations and perspectives is a pivotal strength of this book. Among the four co-authors, one is a European living in Malawi, and another is a Northeast Indian migrant in the UK. They are uniquely positioned to tackle the issues the book raises, including mass migration, a subject often discussed as a crisis, especially in the global North. All of them are involved in theological education in different settings. They come together to present an ecumenical reimagining of mission grounded in a trinitarian theology of unity. This captivating book will undoubtedly enlighten and broaden the understanding of ecumenists, church leaders, professors, and students in theological programs worldwide of the nature of the challenges we all face, pointing to an alternative way to move forward.

Dr. Raimundo Barreto Jr., Princeton Theological Seminary,
New Jersey, USA

Preface

We are living in troubled times as we all face grave and interlocking crises. "It's difficult to convey just how strange life in the third decade of the third millennium has become," writes the former chief book critic of *The New York Times*, Michiko Kakutani, "It often feels like a preposterous mash-up of political satire, disaster movie, reality show, and horror film tropes all at once."[1] In this book we seek to engage with the many-sided crisis of the mid-2020s by turning to what might at first seem a surprising source: the ecumenical mission movement. Our collaboration originated from a project undertaken by the World Council of Churches' Commission on World Mission and Evangelism, commemorating the centenary of the International Missionary Council formed in 1921.[2] This global initiative involved fourteen study centers across every continent, each providing unique insights.[3] The IMC celebration study process unearthed the profound role of missionary work over a hundred years in shaping cultural and ethnic identities, prompting deep reflections on mission and culture, racism, political governance, and the pathways to reconciliation and healing—themes critically relevant to today's global crises. This encouraged us to write this book collectively, applying what we learned from the study process to engage with the challenges of a world in crisis in the mid-2020s.

1. Kakutani, *Great Wave*, 23–24.

2. See World Council of Churches' books on the *International Missionary Council Centenary*: Jukko, *Together in the Mission of God*; Jukko, *Hundred Years of Mission Cooperation*; Jukko, *Future of Mission Cooperation*.

3. So far five volumes of the series publishing the results of the study process have appeared: Robert et al., *Creative Collaborations*; Jamir and Lalrinthanga, *Transformative Rethinking*; van Saane and Holdsworth, *Christian Mission in the Middle East*; Sonea et al., *Heritage of Mission Today*. Forthcoming in 2025: Johannes Knoetze et al., *Missional Encounters of Churches in Sub-Saharan Africa through Grassroots Stories*.

Preface

The distinctive contribution we hope to bring with this book is to retrieve the intertwining of mission and unity that ignited and catalyzed the ecumenical movement a hundred years ago. It is our attempt to delve into the underpinnings of mission and unity that were central to the movement's spirit and evaluate their relevance for the church and the world today. Our exploration considers how these principles can shape a future-oriented vision of mission infused with hope; to unpack the thinking about mission and unity that formed the inner soul of the ecumenical movement and explore what it might mean today not only for the church but especially for its service to the world.

Our approach blends appreciative inquiry with a critical perspective, acknowledging the strengths of the ecumenical tradition while addressing the complicities of churches and missions in destructive historical patterns. Through a creative engagement with the heritage of ecumenical thought, we reimagine possibilities for our collective future. The book confronts the injustices and destructive forces of the contemporary world order without faltering, offering a message of hope that hinges on rejuvenating the ecumenical vision as a beacon for a brighter future.

No one is really able to paint a full picture of the whole world, but we are convinced that we address issues which are representative of the experience of the life of the majority of the people on the globe, although to differing degrees. The selection and progression of the subsequent chapters are designed to expose some of the economic, political, and cultural forces that are currently plunging the world into crisis and to retrieve how the ecumenical mission movement has been addressing comparable issues in earlier decades. This leads us to a chapter discussing the people we believe we need to become and to another on how to understand the role of being missionary in a new way. Our collaborative approach extends to practical strategies for education and formation and to challenging a prevailing complacency that we detect in the understanding and practice of the ecumenical movement and in mission. It prompts an alternative movement, working from a basis in ecumenical Christianity to make common cause with people of all faiths and no-faith who share similar convictions and concerns. The chapter on the triune God offers a perspective from which we move to the hope we need to imagine in order to be empowered to engage in mission in a way that can meet our contemporary crises. This leads in conclusion to our reimagining of ecumenical mission.

Preface

We are aware that it is unusual for a book to have four authors. This is not an anthology with single authors for the different chapters. Instead, through much online interaction and two intensive weekends in Hamburg, in December 2023 and June 2024, we have written all the chapters together. Chapters 2–10 start with a section where we talk to each other, which might give some flavor of the conversations out of which the book has emerged. We hope that the themes we introduce in the successive chapters will draw our readers into conversations of decisive importance for our common future.

1

A World in Crisis

DURING THE LATE TWENTIETH century it seemed to observers, particularly in the Western countries, that international bodies like the United Nations or the European Union were creating greater understanding among the nations and reducing the chances of conflict. After the end of the political block system in 1989, the confident expectation arose that the situation of the world would become better if the nations would join hands. The Sustainable Development Goals (SDG) project of the United Nations is an expression of this confidence. The UN challenged the countries of the world to cooperate and to be committed to a set of positive developments: zero poverty, zero hunger, good health and well-being; quality education; gender equality; clean water and sanitation; affordable and clean energy; decent work and economic growth; industry, innovation, and infrastructure; reduced inequalities; sustainable cities and communities; responsible consumption and production; climate action; life below water; life on land; peace, justice, and strong institutions. The SDGs express the hope that humanity is able to solve the global problems it has itself created if the nations join in partnership.[1]

The SDGs seem to be the global mission of the first half of the twenty-first century, to which most of the churches in the ecumenical movement subscribe.[2] The COVID-19 pandemic, however, made the cracks and fissures of the global situation obvious and demonstrated how vulnerable life is and how global entanglements add to its vulnerability. Even the progress

1. United Nations, "Transforming Our World."
2. *Called to Transformation*, 17, 55–57.

which had been made in alleviating hunger and poverty was crushed under the impact of the regulations imposed to fight the virus and more recently by the impact of the war in Ukraine on the accessibility of wheat—worldwide. This war resulted in, for example, people in Cairo not being able to pay for their daily bread.

Such a connection points to the fact that the divisions and conflicts in our world need a consciousness or awareness. Crises are not automatically understood just by the state of affairs. Someone must collect the information, analyze it, and bring an interpretation into the public discourse in order to understand that we are dealing with a global crisis in which diverse crises interact. The *Collins Dictionary* declared "permacrisis" as the word of the year in 2022.[3] The former chief book critic of *The New York Times* Michiko Kakutani recently characterized our times as the era of radical disruption: "A confluence of crises, both immediate and long-term, has made the military acronym VUCA—meaning volatility, uncertainty, complexity and ambiguity—feel like a perfect description of the third decade of the third millennium."[4]

Instead of the military inspired acronym we prefer the term "hyper-complexity" which describes the intricate interactions and feedback loops between various crises, including but not limited to migration, climate change, authoritarian regimes, political instability, and economic disparities. Hyper-complexity underscores the interconnectedness, the multidimensional nature and scale of the crises facing the world today resulting in uncertainty and ambiguity of attempts to solve them. The term is emphasized to indicate the scale of the challenges and to remind us that coping with crises is not only to address the state of affairs but also the concomitant reasoning and conflicting interpretations and proposals to solve the crises. One particular dimension of our consciousness of today's crises is that the capacity of reason itself seems to be called into question when we consider how we might overcome the crises. If the capacity to discern a crisis comes with the questioning whether the capacity of reason is comprehensive enough, it becomes at least questionable whether reason will be able to recognize opportunities in it.

We ask ourselves, where to look for approaches and solutions in such a hyper-complex situation and what can be done to address them? One

---

3. Bushby, "Permacrisis Declared Collins Dictionary Word of the Year."
4. Kakutani, *Great Wave*, xi.

answer, it seems to us, is to look into the history of the modern mission and ecumenical movement.

The modern Western missionary movement was certainly not free from nationalistic pride or cultural arrogance and its theologies were tainted by racism. In its time it was also a significant force in the development of interconnection and mutual understanding between people from different nations. The missionaries were motivated by confidence in the message they carried but also by the need to identify with and understand the people among whom they lived their lives. Looking back one can recognize that their world was also ridden by complex crises to which they answered with the attempt to found and promote international institutions and cooperation. The missionary movement was always a movement in times of crises and the attempt to cope with them from a Christian perspective became one contributory factor in the emergence of internationalism in modern times. Joe Oldham, the first secretary of the International Missionary Council, formed in 1921, became a pivotal figure in the ecumenical missionary movement that emerged during the early part of the twentieth century. Oldham was keenly aware that he was breaking new ground in building an international platform on which the missions could develop their cooperation. As he stimulated and coordinated the ecumenical movement of missions and churches that ultimately found institutional expression in the World Council of Churches (WCC), he was conscious that his life's work was also connected to the political movement that would give rise, contemporaneously, to the League of Nations and later to the United Nations and related bodies after the Second World War.[5]

Notwithstanding some deeply problematic aspects of the mission movement, looking back and historically speaking, mission seems to have done well. Today it is a global but diverse movement as it will be demonstrated in this volume. But what about its future and challenges? In the 2020s and beyond, mission is facing new challenges. Some of the issues are still, of course, the same as they have always been, i.e., how to witness to Christ in the best possible ways in various contexts around the world. Jesus's words are as valid as they have always been: Christians are witnesses of Christ both near and far (Acts 1:8) and to the very end of the age (Matt 28:20). Mission has always met with challenges, and in our time some new challenges are global trends that impact mission and churches everywhere: the so-called global megatrends due to globalization. Aware of the crises,

---

5. See further Clements, *Faith on the Frontier*.

people may fear that we are entering the "last days" and so one dimension of mission is to re-examine the dimension of hope. One glimpse of hope is that already these megatrends have brought churches and missions closer to one another.

CLIMATE CRISIS

Everyone notices the rise of temperature and other effects of climate change. Every year we hear news of extreme heat waves, droughts, forest fires, and floods. Nature has become more unpredictable and its system changes under the ruthless exploitation, damage, and pollution that we humans have done at least during the last five hundred years, in the name of human superiority and welfare, hiding the greediness and selfishness of both individuals and large corporations, enterprises, and countries.

A livable future is threatened by the climate crisis. The International Panel on Climate Change published a synthesis report on climate change in March 2023, stating that "vulnerable communities who have historically contributed the least to current climate change are disproportionately affected."[6] What is urgently needed is international cooperation, in addition to finance and technology. This cooperation is possible through "multiple channels."[7] Churches and mission societies can play a role of critical enabler of accelerated climate action,[8] but they need to discover the urgency and importance of mission cooperation.

Climate scientist Bill McGuire has advised that "the coming decade is very likely the most critical in human history." On his estimation, there is now no way for the world to avoid being hard hit by climate change. The fork in the road is between one way that leads to a "calamitous and unsustainable future," and another that leads to "a world in which rapidly falling emissions have slowed the rate of heating and large-scale adaptation has led to much greater resilience."[9] There is a broad scientific consensus about what needs to be done in order for the world to take the latter path rather than the former. It is also clear, however, that the human community has been unable to motivate and organize itself to take the actions needed to set the world on the second path. This is largely because of the power

---

6. Intergovernmental Panel on Climate Change, "Summary for Policymakers," A2.
7. Intergovernmental Panel on Climate Change, "Summary for Policymakers," C7.
8. *Kairos for Creation*.
9. McGuire, *Hothouse Earth*, 155.

of those who have vested interests in the status quo and are able to resist change. Division and inequality mean that the human community is poorly placed when it comes to meeting the climate crisis. It is already clear that, in the short term, the wealthy can protect themselves from the worst effects of climate change. Those who take the primary impact are the poor and vulnerable.

In a divided world, with nations suspicious and hostile towards one another, and deep polarization within many nations, the first instinct is for people to look after themselves with little concern for those they regard as "others." Such an attitude is reinforced by the neoliberal economic system. As McGuire remarks: "Our climate is being destroyed by unadulterated, free-market capitalism—an ideology that simply cannot be sustained on a small planet with limited resources. It is a system that has no interest in the greater good and that rewards inordinate capital and the few that have it, rather than the majority who don't. It cares nothing for the environment or biodiversity and doesn't give a fig about the fate of future generations. In fact, it is *exactly* the wrong economic system to have in place at a time of global crisis."[10]

It is clear that the human community needs to find an entirely new vision and new way of organizing its shared life on earth. Of course, there are climate activists pressing for a fundamental rethink, but their voices are often marginalized and discounted. Was this concern to be brought to the front and center of the life of the world's religious communities, with their vast extent and profound reach, might this create the momentum for change that is needed?

Though an ethic of caring for the earth is built into many religious traditions, it has too often receded into the background during the modern industrial age. This is certainly the case with Christianity which, through its close alliance with the European Enlightenment, was complicit in the exploitation of the earth's resources that drove the colonial system. In other words, churches and missions need to take God's creation seriously and mission urgently needs to re-think its relationship with nature. This missiological reflection would include at least a new theology of creation and soteriology, i.e., "the relationship between human salvation and the rest of God's creation."[11]

---

10. McGuire, *Hothouse Earth*, 161.

11. Robert, "Historical Trends in Missions and Earth Care," 127. See also for example Conradie, *Earth in God's Economy*.

The Assembly of the WCC, held at Karlsruhe, Germany, in 2022, spoke of the "Living Planet" and urged: "We are all interdependent in God's whole Creation. As Christ's love moves the world to reconciliation and unity, we are called to *metanoia* and a renewed and just relationship with creation that expresses itself in our practical life." It warns that we "are running out of time for this *metanoia* to take place."[12] As Pope Francis suggests, Christians need an "ecological conversion whereby the effects of their encounter with Jesus Christ becomes evident in their relationship to the world around them."[13] His All-Holiness Ecumenical Patriarch Bartholomew, dubbed the "Green Patriarch," made a similar point when he emphasized that "climate change primarily constitutes a spiritual and ethical issue—not only a governmental or technological problem."[14] Such a conversion involves an orientation to both mission and unity—discovering the sense of purpose and commitment needed by an agent of change and discovering that, if we are going to succeed in meeting this unprecedented challenge, we need each other. Here is where the experience and thinking of the ecumenical movement might prove to be a vital resource. Its sense of coming together to undertake a monumental task is needed more than ever if we are to meet the great crisis of our time.

A WORLD AT WAR?

Division and conflict are not new features of human life on earth but their growing intensity during the first decades of the twenty-first century has, for many, been an unpleasant surprise. The Russian invasion of Ukraine in February 2022 might be remembered as one moment marking our entry into a new age of violent division and conflict. At least for Europeans it was a shock to witness scenes reminiscent of the World Wars, only with even more destructive weaponry being deployed. Meanwhile less-noticed wars in such countries as Yemen, South Sudan, and Ethiopia have taken no less a toll in loss of life and human suffering. The conflict in the Middle East irrupted to a new dimension after the Hamas attack in Israel in 2023 and the subsequent Israeli invasion and bombardment of Gaza. Particularly here, we observe one conspicuous dimension of conflicts in the age of globalization. Although they rage in a region, a broad range of countries

---

12. "Living Planet," 175.
13. Pope Francis, *Laudato Si'*, §217.
14. Patriarch Bartholomew, *Address by His All-Holiness*, para. 4.

are involved. They also lead to a polarization between groups and social movements in various countries outside the conflict zone.[15]

In March 2024 Donald Tusk, Polish prime minister and former president of the European Council, warned that Europe is in a "pre-war era": "I don't want to scare anyone but war is no longer a concept from the past."[16] His note of alarm carried credibility because conflict and warfare are becoming normal and expected. As the political commentator Tom Stevenson has grimly observed, "The threat of inter-superstate violence no longer seems as latent as it did. Superstates or no, the five largest economies in the world are all either currently involved in a war, rearming, or making preparations."[17] This means that the threat of nuclear warfare, with its catastrophic effects, is not only theoretical, as was demonstrated in the language used in the Russia-Ukraine conflict.

The problem is, however, that increasing the defense budget will not provide a solution. If anything, it might make matters worse. While war is beneficial for the arms trade which forms a central plank of the economy in several wealthy countries, it invariably has a disastrous effect on the lives of the poor and vulnerable. Pouring resources into military expenditure is also a distraction from the truly serious battle that needs to be fought in our time—resisting destructive climate change. Such is the scale of the climate emergency that all possible resources need to be devoted to the transition to a green economy. The last thing the world needs is wealthy nations arming themselves to fight each other over the resources for survival such as land and water, a fight which has already started.

POLARIZED SOCIETIES

If conflict between nations is an increasing threat, the problem is also found within nations. Throughout the twentieth century the USA appeared to be the epitome of stability and democracy. It presents a very different picture today after disputed elections, an attempted insurrection at the US Capitol on January 6, 2021, and an ever more polarized society. "Where is the United States today?" asks American political scientist Barbara Walter. "We are a factionalised anocracy that is quickly approaching the open insurgency

---

15. Kaldor, *New and Old Wars*.
16. Chiappa, "War Looms for Europe."
17. Stevenson, "Empires in Disguise," 12.

stage."[18] Such deep social divisions, unfortunately, are not confined to the United States but are mirrored in such diverse contexts as Brazil where on January 9, 2023, there was a similar attack on the parliament as in Washington, and in different ways in India and the United Kingdom, to name only those countries from which two of us originate.

Little wonder that in this environment racism is resurgent. It is impressive that many European countries have been hospitable to refugees from the war in Ukraine in 2022–25. Nevertheless, it is hard to miss the contrast between this generous hospitality and the prevailing attitudes to those who have fled no less tragic situations in Afghanistan, Iraq, Somalia, Sudan, and other countries where the prevailing racial identity is black or brown. In a study of the reporting on the war in Ukraine, social commentator Meehan Crist notes the usually unquestioned assumption that the terrible scenes are shocking because they are occurring in Europe whereas such things are to be expected in the non-Western world. She writes that, "The war in Ukraine has served . . . as a reminder of the attitudes of many in the West to the suffering of black and brown people. Implicitly and explicitly, politicians and commentators have made clear their disparagement, their ignorance, their casual cultural supremacy."[19] Institutional racism has been exposed and condemned in the police forces of countries like France, Germany, the USA, and the UK, with the Black Lives Matter movement highlighting the targeting, sometimes fatally, of young men simply on account of their black skin. The fact that such racism is built into the institutions of the state indicates how far we still have to go in the struggle to overcome this false, divisive, and exploitative ideology.[20]

INEQUALITY

A central thrust of the ecumenical vision concerns a sense of common belonging, mutual accountability, and equitable sharing. Those inspired by such a vision cannot rest content in a situation where some are prospering while others are suffering deprivation. When the WCC 2018 Conference on World Mission and Evangelism assessed the global situation, it began by putting its finger on "the shocking accumulation of wealth due to one global financial system, which enriches few and impoverishes many (Isa

---

18. Meek, Review of Walter, *How Civil Wars Start*, 6.
19. Crist, "War in Ukraine," 9.
20. See for example Kwiyani, "Mission After George Floyd."

5:8). This is at the root of many of today's wars, conflicts, ecological devastation, and suffering (1 Tim 6:10)."[21] The point is that such disasters are not just happening by accident or by bad luck. There is a system at work. As the Accra Confession of the World Alliance of Reformed Churches explained in 2004:

This crisis is directly related to the development of neoliberal economic globalization, which is based on the following beliefs:

- unrestrained competition, consumerism, and the unlimited economic growth and accumulation of wealth are the best for the whole world;
- the ownership of private property has no social obligation;
- capital speculation, liberalization and deregulation of the market, privatization of public utilities and national resources, unrestricted access for foreign investments and imports, lower taxes and the unrestricted movement of capital will achieve wealth for all;
- social obligations, protection of the poor and the weak, trade unions, and relationships between people, are subordinate to the processes of economic growth and capital accumulation.[22]

Despite being exposed and resisted by such analysis, the neoliberal global financial system has continued to entrench itself, defended by military might and promoted through its capture of media outlets and political processes worldwide. As a result, this fundamental imbalance and fatal flaw in the functioning of the global economy is worsening year on year. As environmental activist George Monbiot explains, "The underlying problem isn't hard to grasp: governments have failed to break what the economist Thomas Piketty calls the patrimonial spiral of wealth accumulation. As a result, the rich have become ever richer, a process that seems to be accelerating."[23] The political economist Geoff Mann has pointed out that "in the United States . . . an average member of the richest 1 per cent now receives more than eighty times as much income, and owns 950 times as much wealth, as an average member of the bottom 50 per cent."[24] The

---

21. Jukko and Keum, *Moving in the Spirit*, 2.

22. World Alliance of Reformed Churches, *Accra Confession*.

23. Monbiot, "With Our Food Systems on the Verge of Collapse"; Piketty, *Capital in the Twenty-First Century*.

24. Mann, "Inequality Machine," 25.

Scottish health budget is about £4,000 per person, per year; in Malawi the equivalent figure is approximately £10.

Inequality within the human community is becoming not only obscene but manifestly unsustainable. Very different is the biblical vision evoked by the apostle Paul: "The one who gathered much did not have too much, and the one who gathered little did not have too little" (2 Cor 8:15). Against the neoliberal ideology, it is clear that market forces, by themselves, are not able to address the patrimonial spiral, unless we accept that the majority of world population is made to pay the price for its in-built cycle of crises in which a minority can even augment its wealth. Vision and action must come from outside the currently prevailing system. Key values of the hundred-year-old ecumenical movement have been mutual accountability, sharing of resources, and care for one another. Might these values be needed today not only for relations between churches but to inform a rebalancing of the global economy so that there can be a livable future for the human community and the earth itself?

BANKRUPT POLITICS

The climate crisis has exposed the inadequacy of existing political systems to meet the unprecedented challenge that it presents. In most contexts, politics is national and the cycle is short. Often the horizon on which politicians are focused is no further ahead than the next election. All energy is absorbed by maneuvers aimed to secure short-term political advantage. This very much plays against any serious action on climate change since this normally involves some short-term sacrifice with a view to securing a sustainable future in the long term. The problem, however, is by no means confined to failure to seriously address climate change. There is also a general lack of engagement with the big issues that shape people's lives in favor of a preoccupation with petty point-scoring within a political class that is increasingly detached from society at large. No wonder there is widespread disillusionment with politics. As Perry Anderson, a British political philosopher, observes, "in this century . . . political expectations in advanced societies have declined nearly everywhere."[25] "Listless acquiescence," he suggests, is the best that can be expected as political life fails to capture the imagination.

---

25. Anderson, "Ever Closer Union?," 34.

A World in Crisis

Inasmuch as citizens become motivated by political issues, it is all too often the politics of grievance as media funded and controlled by those who stand to benefit from fomenting social division try to influence public opinion. Social media opened a space not only for polarizing communities by hate speech and fake news, but also for large scale campaigns orchestrated to influence votes. Resorting to culture wars has become a familiar tactic on the part of unsuccessful governments that are failing to get to grips with the issues they face. The malaise, however, extends far beyond the professional politicians who operate at national level. The former editor of the *Times Literary Supplement* Ferdinand Mount notes, for example, the shrinking role of trade unions, the huge drop in the membership numbers of political parties, the decreasing influence of business organizations, and the diminishing role of impartial broadcasters.[26] Organizations fighting for common interests seem to have been replaced by platforms that provide space for the articulation of common outrage which puts pressure on agents. Space for political imagination and initiative has been severely narrowed down. Politics and the media through which it is expressed are trivialized.

From where will politics find its renewal? The ecumenical movement has consistently looked from a faith perspective at the times in which we live, offering critique, perspective, and hope. While it has no aim or intention to supplant political life, as a global network it is well placed to inform it about the remotest places, to remind it of ultimate issues, and to inspire people to unite around a common transnational political purpose with a long-time perspective. Extraordinary political will and an unusual degree of unity is needed if there is to be any realistic hope of overcoming crises that threaten to engulf our human society. A renewed ecumenical mission movement is one resource that needs to be mobilized.

THE HUMAN PERSON

The secular turn in human society, particularly evident in the Western world, has significant positive features and has also brought a needed critique to the way in which Christianity has been understood during its many centuries at the heart of Western communities. At the same time, the limitations of the secular vision are becoming ever more apparent. It is doubtful today both whether it can satisfy the inner longings that are constitutive of human identity and whether it can unify people in the way that is needed

---

26. Mount, "Après Brexit," 9.

to forge a common future. Amidst all the other crises, there is a crisis of the human person. How can we discover our true human identity and vocation? Such questions, fundamentally religious, have not gone away.

But challenges also abound in non-Western societies. The reasons, why someone is considered as an enemy often enough are based on political, social, and economic reasons but ideologized in religious terms. In India, for example, tribals and their ways of life including their religion are declared to be backward and genocide takes place, legitimized in the name of development towards modernity.[27] Economic and political arguments are translated into the cultural and religious space and used to legitimize action against certain groups. The WCC mission affirmation *Together Towards Life* (TTL) speaks about the "excessive assertion of religious identities and persuasions that seem to break and brutalize in the name of God rather than heal and nurture communities."[28]

One thing that the ecumenical movement has discovered, through its hundred-year experience, is that there is a relational quality to human life. The deeper we can go in our relations to one another, especially to those with whom we have had differences, the greater our discovery of what our human personhood means. The missionary and ecumenical leader John Taylor observed that "the word *allelous*—one another—rings through the pages of the New Testament like a peal of bells."[29] This led him to suggest that "every opening of one's whole self towards another, every taking upon oneself the burden and the gift of another, contributes a little to that quiet tide which is flowing back and forth, carrying us with it into the very being of God, sweeping us back with God into the life of the world."[30] Such is the ecumenical vision—it is in finding our place in the flowing of this tide that our human identity and vocation can be found.

A particular challenge at the present time, with all its painful experiences and apparently intractable challenges, is the question of how we can live our lives with any measure of contentment, not to mention joy. To claim to have found happiness and fulfillment when the world around us is ravaged by warfare and threatened by climate crisis could easily seem to be nothing more than false consciousness. However, Jürgen Moltmann, the globally renowned German reformed theologian, suggests love as a secret

---

27. Padel, "In the Name of Sustainable Development."
28. Keum, *Together Towards Life*, §82.
29. Wood, *Poet, Priest and Prophet*, 204.
30. Wood, *Poet, Priest and Prophet*, 210.

answer to this troubling question of life: "In love we go out of ourselves and lay ourselves open to all the experiences of life. In the love of life we become happy and vulnerable at the same time. In love we can be happy and sad. In love we can laugh and weep. In love we can rejoice and must protest at the same time. The more deeply love draws us into life, the more alive and, simultaneously, the more capable of sorrow we become."[31] Such love speaks of deep humanity and indicates the direction in which our true human personhood is to be found.

MISSION A MATTER OF THE SPIRIT

The rethinking of ecumenical mission that has been taking place during the early twenty-first century has needed a large canvas on which to work. It has found fresh coherence around the multivalent concept of "life," as indicated in the title of the groundbreaking mission affirmation *Together Towards Life*. This document, approved by the 354 member churches of the WCC and thus by all the major confessional families, brings together their reflection on mission, unity, and ecumenical communion in changing landscapes.[32] New awareness that life itself is at stake has given renewed urgency to mission and a fresh vitality to the ecumenical impulse. This has prompted a turn to creation theology and, in particular, to an innovative integration of mission and the flourishing of creation (§§19–23). It has also prompted a pneumatological turn in mission thinking: understanding mission in terms of the Spirit of God. For our reflection on ecumenical mission this is an important resource, particularly in pointing us to mission as a matter of the Spirit.

Rather than thinking of mission in terms of institutions or strategies, TTL proposes that "life in the Holy Spirit is the essence of mission, the core of why we do what we do and how we live our lives. Spirituality gives the deepest meaning to our lives and motivates our actions. It is a sacred gift from the Creator, the energy for affirming and caring for life" (§3). In this perspective, mission is not so much a project as a way of being, a way of living. In a world crying out for authenticity, people of faith are challenged to demonstrate their identity and vocation in the way they live. This in turn creates an openness among people of all faiths and none, shared humanity

---

31. Moltmann, "Christianity," 14.

32. Keum, *Together Towards Life*. The paragraphs quoted in the text refer to the document.

bringing them together and breaking down barriers. Such an expansive approach will be needed if the challenges facing our world today are to be met.

Mission can be understood in many different ways. In the ecumenical movement a decisive insight has been that it is never *our* mission; always it is the mission of God. And we are invited to be part of it. As TTL puts it, "By the Spirit we participate in the mission of God that is at the heart of the life of the Trinity." This is both humbling and empowering. It results, the document continues, "in Christian witness which unceasingly proclaims the salvific power of God through Jesus Christ and constantly affirms God's dynamic involvement, through the Holy Spirit, in the whole created world." (§18). This opens up a broad, dynamic, and relational field in which to fulfill a vocation. Rather than thinking of mission as a competitive or aggressive enterprise that aims to "defeat" people of other faiths, TTL suggests that "in doing evangelism it is important to build relations and trust between people of different faiths" (§110). Such relations and such trust will surely prove vital at a time when there is need for the human community not to break apart but to pull together in meeting grave threats to its very existence.

However, it is also a marker for the discussion on who defines what theology and mission theology look like (or need to look like) and can give some input to the Spirit theology. TTL, for example, twice mentions indigenous peoples (§43, §65) in a generic way and includes many references to the presence of the Spirit in cultures, religions, and in the history of peoples.

Even though there is a self-critical tonality and the call for *metanoia* is voiced, many passages of the WCC mission documents are written as if the church is the sanctuary of holiness. Mission theology has to start from the consciousness of the unavoidable involvement in the current situation. We pray to be part of the solution and to become a force for transformation—but we must admit that we are implicated in the powers that have created the current state of affairs.

RENEWAL OF ECUMENICAL VISION

It appears that the world is crying out for some new vision and unifying purpose—some guiding light that would show the way out of what threatens to become a very dark place. This book points to a source of vision and hope that at first sight might look unlikely. The ecumenical movement that inspired churches in the middle years of the twentieth century seemed to have run out of steam by the end of it. In many places dreams of church union came to nothing and even the instruments of ecumenical cooperation declined or even disappeared. Yet this book will argue that the world today needs the ecumenical impulse that moved church leaders to strive to come closer to one another and find common purpose rather than cultivating mutual suspicion and competition. Can we learn from one hundred years of ecumenical endeavor on the part of the churches? In the following chapters we identify leading visions and activities driven by hope in the ecumenical movement, joining in God's mission and in discerning the presence of the Spirit in the midst of the daunting challenges. Our hope is that the lessons learned might be relevant not only for the churches themselves but also for the entire human community and its problems. Can the memory of such moments confirm memories such as the psalmists are recalling in order to find strength and resilience in the midst of the threat of death (see Ps 9:8–10; Ps 77:11–12, passim)?

A renewal of ecumenical mission theology could be significant not only for churches and missions but also for international relations at a time of fragmentation and conflict. Such a renewal needs to critically engage the dimension of coloniality in mission, both in history and in the present. It needs efforts to create decolonizing mission theology to show that mission being God's mission was more than a tool in the hands of human colonizers. We are convinced that critical missiological work and decolonializing studies paint such a more nuanced and critical picture. We do not subscribe to every expression of mission and are critical of various aspects of what is happening currently under the heading of mission. However, the fact that mission today is a global movement and that many of such critiques and studies come from those who could be considered as victims of the colonial history and who continue to find strength and hope in God's mission among them[33] confirms our conviction that mission has not only a past, but a future. Reckoning with the past challenges, those engaging in mission need to be transformed to become authentic disciples, as has been spelled out in the wake of the jubilee conference Edinburgh 2010[34] and at the World Mission Conference at Arusha in 2018.[35]

---

33. See for example the contributions in the issue "Mission and Decolonization" of the *International Review of Mission*, November 2023.

34. Ma and Ross, *Mission Spirituality and Authentic Discipleship*.

35. Jukko and Keum, *Moving in the Spirit*.

One crucial feature of the ecumenical movement that calls for retrieval is that it was the missionary dimension of the Christian faith that ignited it. As people were inspired by their faith to look outwards, to glimpse the unfolding of the purpose of God in human history and to seek to be part of it, they found themselves being drawn to one another and impelled to work for cooperation and unity. These two—mission and unity—were like two sides of a coin. You could not have the one without the other. Today, many would agree that our world is in need of mission in the sense that the way the human community is operating needs to become different from the way things are now. Therefore, there is a need for agents of change—"missionaries." This is not any narrowly conceived mission for it is as wide as the presence of God and as broad as the purposes of God. This book is written from a Christian perspective, and it is open to the adventure of discerning the action of the Spirit of God who constantly takes us by surprise. Far from promoting an exclusive, intolerant, or bigoted approach to others, this missionary orientation forms people who are open, curious, and eager to make common cause in resisting the forces that make for death and embracing those that make for life.

FUTURE AND HOPE

In order to understand and adapt and react better to the challenges presented above, mission studies have always been interdisciplinary, and one discipline to which mission studies has resorted is social sciences. Missiological study of the future can use, for example, future studies researcher Sohail Inayatullah's model.[36] He has proposed that in the study of the future aiming at transformation we need to look at the past, the present, and the future. First, mission needs to look at the past. We need to consider what are continuities in our Christian heritage that we must not lose, and what are discontinuities that we may lose, even need to give up. This kind of reflection on mission will help us to become clearer in which direction to go in the future, even if the history of mission has a certain weight and pulls us down in our efforts, together with the negative sides of the mentioned megatrends. These weights are barriers to the future that prevent our creativity and imagination from the future as we would like to see.

In this book we hope to contribute to identifying lessons learned and to look forward by reflecting on the present. A part of missiological reflection

36. Inayatullah, "Six Pillars."

on future is, not surprisingly, the present. What is happening today is affecting our decisions for tomorrow. Mission studies has used statistics for a long time. If we look at the Report of the World Missionary Conference in Edinburgh 1910, we find tables and figures, i.e., statistics. David Barrett is often—and rightly—referred to when mission barometers are considered.[37] But a missiological reflection on the future does not limit itself to numbers of missionaries, or Christians, or churches, or religions in the world. It is at least interested in other trends, for example world population, its birth rates and aging, GNP and GDP, development aid and military spending, climate change, etc. Those are some factors that are influential and decisive in contexts where mission is taking place today. They, and a reflection on them, should inspire and push mission to a more plausible future.

And then comes the future.[38] It is clear to Christians that the future is God's future (Jer 29:11; cf. Heb 13:8). However, this does not mean that mission should not reflect on, and think of, the future—on the contrary. Thinking of the future, at least four levels, or approaches, can be distinguished.[39] The first is the level of survival. Western churches and mission societies seem to be happy to continue their missionary work as they have always done, starting from the same presumptions as in the eighteenth, nineteenth, and twentieth centuries. Because of a relatively successful story, there seems to be no incentive, or courage, to change anything in the twenty-first century. Change seems to happen only when there is no other alternative. But non-Western churches and missions with shorter histories are faced with the same risk.

The second level of thinking of future includes a use of strategy. In this approach mission leaders are ready to think strategically about its goals and consequently to change its structures to be more responsive, inclusive, and adapted to global challenges of the twenty-first century. The practical role of the church in mission has to be defined in each context, as each context is different. A strategy will enhance the mission work and create its credibility as an organizational response to the global challenges.

The third level is the global challenges, some of which are presented above. These form the big picture that mission needs to have. It necessitates capable mission leaders and mission theologians to perceive and

---

37. Zurlo, *From Nairobi to the World*.

38. These three periods and the reflection based on them can happen simultaneously even if we present them here in a chronological order.

39. Inayatullah, "Six Pillars," 8.

understand the broader social context in which they are working or which they are observing. It means being ambitious enough to climb up to the mountain top to see the whole picture of mission in their contexts, remembering at the same time that global is also local.

The fourth level of reflection on future is a vision. "Where there is no vision the people perish," says Prov 29:18 poignantly.[40] In the same way as the wise men in the Gospel according to Matthew saw a star in the east and followed it (Matt 2:1–12), mission needs a vision for the future. It is not enough to stay on the day-to-day survival level, it is not enough to have an updated strategy, as good as it may be, and it is not even enough to have a glimpse at the big picture. Mission needs all of them. It needs to survive from day to day, but based on a strategy which leans on a good understanding of the broader social context in which it operates but, above all, it needs a vision, a "star in the east" to follow and move forward. This may mean developing alternative scenarios of future, or different assumptions of how the world may look like in the future, and in particular, of course, how the church may look like in the future and what the next appropriate steps are to go in that direction.

Following such an approach to connect past, present, and future reignites exploration of the concept of hope. An ecumenical vision of hope provides a lens through which mission can be both reimagined and enacted in the midst of daunting challenges. In this context, hope serves as a critical theological resource that motivates and sustains mission.

---

40. In this case we choose the KJV translation because the verse has entered ordinary language in this rendering.

2

The Earth We Need to Cherish

Marina: Kenneth, you are living in Zomba, Malawi. What kind of place is it?

Kenneth: It is a small city nestled in the foothills of Zomba Mountain which rises above it to around six thousand feet. In colonial times it was the capital city. Today it is still a military town but has also developed as an educational center, with schools and universities. In the peri-urban and nearby rural areas there are many smallholder farmers.

Marina: What happened there in March 2023?

Kenneth: We were hit by Cyclone Freddy, the most intense tropical storm ever recorded by meteorologists in the southern hemisphere.

Marina: My goodness! What was that like for you?

Kenneth: It was a strange time. Our university, along with all schools in our area, was closed and we were advised to stay at home to keep safe. So, for three days I was just at home looking out at the torrential rain and gusts of wind. Then we started to hear disturbing reports of its effects.

Marina: What was happening?

Kenneth: Much devastation. Many houses fell down, often causing injuries to their occupants and leaving many homeless. More than forty bridges were swept away so many people were cut off and relief agencies could not easily reach them. Worst of all, landslides came crashing down hills and mountains, destroying everything in their path. In some places whole villages were swept away. Many people were buried in the mud, which became an unplanned graveyard. It was like the apocalyptic scenes described in the Bible when mountains fall on people, but it was happening here and now.

Marina: It is hard to imagine how this could happen so suddenly. What was it like afterwards?

Kenneth: Very sadly it was found that more than six hundred people had been killed and some five hundred others were missing. The Malawi Government estimated that 659,278 people were displaced, many of them finding refuge in the 576 camps that were quickly established, often based around churches or schools. Many others saw some or all of their crops destroyed before they could be harvested, which meant severe food shortages in the year ahead. The positive side was that there was a huge effort to help those who had been adversely affected—every neighborhood and every institution did what they could, as well as national and international agencies. A massive rebuilding program quickly got underway.

Marina: How can you explain such a sudden and devastating event?

Kenneth: Malawi has known some very destructive storms earlier in its history, but today's climate change is bringing severe storms with greater frequency and intensity. Most of those who lost their lives or saw their properties swept away have contributed very little to the causes of climate change. Yet they are the ones bearing the brunt of its impact.

Marina: Is there anything that can be done to prevent such a tragedy happening again?

Kenneth: There are local actions that can help. For example, the deforestation of mountains and hills increases the chance of landslides so tree planting can be a positive initiative. But to a great extent Malawi's future depends on whether or not there can be effective action at a global level to counter destructive climate change.

Marina: From Malawi's perspective what needs to be done?

Kenneth: Malawi's experience tells us that the climate crisis is upon us now. Promises to take action by 2030 or 2050 are not good enough. As a matter of urgency, there needs to be an unprecedented international effort that reconfigures the global economy, tackles the underlying causes of climate change, and protects those most vulnerable to climate catastrophe.

THE CRISIS

THE DEVASTATING EXPERIENCE OF people in southern Malawi, unfortunately, is not unusual in today's world. Many communities are being hit by storms, droughts, floods, wildfires, and other effects of extreme weather. These are not just random events. There is an underlying cause. The earth's atmosphere is changing in ways that are hostile to the natural environment and to the human community. The evidence becomes ever more incontrovertible. Temperatures are increasing, sea levels are rising, devastating weather events are becoming more common, biodiversity is declining at an unprecedented rate, water is becoming more contaminated, more and more plastics are entering the food chain. As a result, many are compelled to leave their homes which have become inhospitable. Globally, 2023 was the hottest year ever recorded.[1] A recent study found that "at current rates of soil degradation . . . the world on average has sixty more years of harvests."[2] As Pope Francis observed in October 2023, The world in which we live is collapsing and may be nearing the breaking point."[3]

The catastrophic climate change that defines our time is not mysterious or unexplained. Sound scientific work has demonstrated that it is human activity that is causing it. Specifically, it is the human activity, primarily extraction and burning of fossil fuels, that releases greenhouse gases into the atmosphere and causes global warming. As the Intergovernmental Panel on Climate Change (IPCC) reported early in 2023: "Human activities, principally through emissions of greenhouse gases, have unequivocally caused global warming, with global surface temperature reaching 1.1°C above 1850–1900 in 2011–2020."[4] The number 1.1 might sound small, but the IPCC points out the devastating effects of this trend: "Widespread and rapid changes in the atmosphere, ocean, cryosphere and biosphere have occurred. Human-caused climate change is already affecting many weather and climate extremes in every region across the globe."[5]

If things are bad, they are also set to become a lot worse very soon. A 2023 Oxfam report warns that unless we rapidly reduce carbon emissions, we will exhaust the amount of carbon we can emit without triggering

---

1. Report of the Copernicus Climate Change Service, cited in Niranjan, "2023 on Track to Be the Hottest Year on Record, Say Scientists."
2. Monbiot, *Out of the Wreckage*, 117.
3. Pope Francis, *Laudate Deum*, §2.
4. Intergovernmental Panel on Climate Change, "Summary for Policymakers," 4.
5. Intergovernmental Panel on Climate Change, "Summary for Policymakers," 5.

climate breakdown within just five years.⁶ All the evidence confirms that global warming poses a clear and present danger to life on earth and yet we continue down the same road. No wonder author and social activist Naomi Klein is moved to ask: "What is wrong with us?"⁷ The climate crisis not only poses sharp questions about the future of the environment. It asks us searching questions about ourselves.

As Orthodox Ecumenical Patriarch Bartholomew has repeatedly emphasized climate change constitutes a spiritual and ethical issue.

> Orthodox theology takes a further step and recognizes the natural creation as inseparable from the identity and destiny of humanity, because every human action leaves a lasting imprint on the body of the earth. Human attitudes and behaviour toward creation directly impact on and reflect human attitudes and behaviour toward other people. Ecology is inevitably related in both its etymology and its meaning to economy; our global economy is simply outgrowing the capacity of our planet to support it. At stake is not just our ability to live in a sustainable way but our very survival.⁸

Since the Rio Earth Summit in 1992, the United Nations has provided an annual forum to enable the nations of the earth to come together to address the climate crisis. These annual summits have reached some landmark agreements but, unfortunately, these have a strong track record of not being implemented. For example, a review of the historic Paris Agreements of 2015 revealed that by 2021 none of the G20 countries had plans in place to meet their commitments.⁹ The stark reality, as Oxfam reported in 2023, is that "the G20—both collectively, and almost all of them individually—are failing to achieve their fair share of ambitious global mitigation required to limit global temperature increase to 1.5°C."¹⁰

A primary responsibility of any elected government is the protection of its citizens. It is now very obvious that climate change represents a clear and present danger to the life and welfare of those citizens. Yet it appears that no government has been able to take the action that would be required to offer convincing protection. There is a highly disturbing contrast between the scale and urgency of the problem and the feebleness and lethargy with

---

6. Oxfam, *Climate Equality*, xiii.
7. Klein, *This Changes Everything*, 15.
8. Patriarch Bartholomew, "Wonder of Creation and Ecology," 126.
9. Frankopan, *Earth Transformed*, 16–17.
10. Oxfam, *Are G20 Countries Doing Their Fair Share of Global Climate Mitigation?*, 5.

which governments are approaching it. It is difficult to resist the conclusion that they are not serious, and their attention is elsewhere. As Pope Francis observes: "Regrettably, the climate crisis is not exactly a matter that interests the great economic powers, whose concern is with the greatest profit possible at minimal cost and in the shortest amount of time."[11] Patriarch Bartholomew emphasized the direct link between ecological problems and poverty so that "all ecological activity is ultimately measured and properly judged by its impact and effect upon the poor (Matthew 25)."[12] Yet, as the 2023 IPCC report underlines: "There is a rapidly closing window of opportunity to secure a liveable and sustainable future for all."[13]

Lip service is paid to the issue of global warming and international meetings are held with great fanfare. But to what effect? Naomi Klein suggests that "the annual U.N. climate summit, which remains the best hope for a political breakthrough on climate action, has started to seem less like a forum for serious negotiation than a very costly and high-carbon group therapy session, a place for representatives of the most vulnerable countries in the world to vent their grief and rage while low-level representatives of the nations largely responsible for their tragedies stare at their shoes."[14] The crisis is not only about the harm caused to the atmosphere by human action in the past and present. It is also about the failure of the human community to take decisive action to prevent things becoming very much worse in the future.

THE RETHINK

The twenty-first century has seen a growing awareness worldwide of the issues presented by climate change. Governments make pledges and introduce policies designed to resist the advance of damaging climate change. Commercial companies are motivated to adopt measures that align them with a progressive green agenda. Individuals adjust their lifestyle choices so as to reduce their carbon footprint. No one could credibly claim that the climate crisis has been completely ignored. Nevertheless, it is clear that the growing awareness and the well-intentioned actions have not been sufficient to resist the advance and acceleration of damaging climate change.

11. Pope Francis, *Laudate Deum*, §13.
12. Patriarch Bartolomew, "Wonder of Creation and Ecology," 126.
13. Intergovernmental Panel on Climate Change, "Summary for Policymakers," 24.
14. Klein, *This Changes Everything*, 11.

Have we too easily settled for tokenism when a much more fundamental rethink is required?

Since the Industrial Revolution that began in Europe in the eighteenth century, humankind has been geared to take an extractivist approach to the earth and its resources. Extracting coal and oil to provide power for industry and to support the modern way of life has come to define our relationship to natural resources—to the extent that it is difficult to imagine anything different. Hence even when it is demonstrated beyond any reasonable doubt that the extraction and use of fossil fuels is the primary cause of catastrophic climate change, we continue to expand and develop fossil fuel industries. What is required now is not just a slow and steady introduction of more renewable energy. Rapid and radical action is called for, particularly in phasing out the use of fossil fuels as a matter of urgency. For this to occur there needs to be a change in our whole way of thinking about our relationship with the earth and the generation of energy. "The challenge," writes Naomi Klein, "is not simply that we need to spend a lot of money and change a lot of policies; it's that we need to think differently, radically differently, for those changes to be remotely possible."[15]

An exploitative and extractivist mindset needs to give way to one driven by a sense of mutuality, stewardship, and care. In his 2023 apostolic exhortation *Laudate Deum* Pope Francis put his finger on what has gone wrong: "Without a doubt, the natural resources required by technology, such as lithium, silicon and so many others, are not unlimited, yet the greater problem is the ideology underlying an obsession: to increase human power beyond anything imaginable, before which nonhuman reality is a mere resource at its disposal. Everything that exists ceases to be a gift for which we should be thankful, esteem and cherish, and instead becomes a slave, prey to any whim of the human mind and its capacities."[16] There is need for a new humility in understanding the place of humanity within the wider creation and a new appreciation of how much is at stake in the responsible stewardship of natural resources.

In this regard it must be acknowledged that Christianity has more often been part of the problem than part of the solution.[17] While Christians have always confessed that the world is the creation of God, this has too

---

15. Klein, *This Changes Everything*, 23.

16. Pope Francis, *Laudate Deum* §22. Compare "Living Planet."

17. This was demonstrated in a seminal article by White, "Historical Roots of Our Ecologic Crisis."

often remained at the periphery of their faith commitment. Their focus has been on the salvation offered to humankind through the coming, dying, and rising of Jesus Christ and the new inter-human relationships that this makes possible. Questions concerning the salvation and reconciliation of human beings were abstracted from the earth from which they draw their life. Concern for the integrity of the natural order was not prominent in the worship and proclamation of the churches. Meanwhile, Western Christianity was closely allied to a colonial commercial enterprise that sought to make profit from new resources and new markets with little thought for the future of the environment. Today's ecological crisis has provoked a profound rethinking of the meaning of Christian faith.

This was demonstrated by the 2012 mission affirmation of the World Council of Churches (WCC), *Together Towards Life* (TTL), when it called for the integration of two spheres of thought that have often been kept apart: missionary commitment and care for creation. It stated the matter in theological terms: "Mission is the overflow of the infinite love of the Triune God. God's mission begins with the act of creation. Creation's life and God's life are entwined. The mission of God's Spirit encompasses us all in an ever-giving act of grace. We are therefore called to move beyond a narrowly human-centered approach and to embrace forms of mission which express our reconciled relationship with all created life."[18] The WCC World Mission Conference held at Arusha in 2018 echoed this concern: "To be worthy missionary disciples we need to be open to the wonder and mystery of creation, transformed by its beauty and called to action by its suffering. God has given us the responsibility to care for the earth, its natural resources and our environment."[19]

This new theological orientation calls for a rethinking of many aspects of Christian faith, including the question of salvation. In one of its most prophetic passages, TTL states:

> We want to affirm our spiritual connection with creation, yet the reality is that the earth is being polluted and exploited. Consumerism triggers not limitless growth but rather endless exploitation of the earth's resources. Human greed is contributing to global warming and other forms of climate change. If this trend continues and earth is fatally damaged, what can we imagine salvation to be? Humanity cannot be saved alone while the rest of the created

---

18. Keum, *Together Towards Life*, §19.
19. "Arusha Conference Report," 11.

world perishes. Eco-justice cannot be separated from salvation, and salvation cannot come without a new humility that respects the needs of all life on earth.[20]

The Arusha Conference underlined the sacrificial commitment that this entails: "If evangelism is to bring good news today, it needs to entail the *kenosis* that puts the long-term sustainability of the earth ahead of our own short-term comfort and convenience."[21]

NOT JUST ONE MONSTER, BUT TWO

It has long been apparent that while the climate crisis jeopardizes the future of everyone, the immediacy and severity of the threat is not shared equally. Nor have all made an equal contribution to the causes of the crisis. As the New Economics Foundation pointed out as early as 2003, "An American family will use more fossil fuel between the stroke of midnight on New Year's Eve and dinnertime on 2 January than a Tanzanian family will use in the entire year."[22] This knowledge is not new. However, it was a groundbreaking Oxfam report published in November 2023 on the eve of the UN Climate Summit in Dubai that revealed just how interlinked the issues of climate breakdown and economic inequality are. The research informing the report, based on collaborative work with the Stockholm Environment Institute, produced stark results.

In 2019, the super-rich 1 percent (77 million people) were responsible for 16 percent of global carbon emissions. This is the same proportion as the emissions of the poorest 66 percent of humanity—a total of 5 billion people. Since the 1990s, the super-rich 1 percent burned through twice as much of the carbon budget as the poorest half of humanity combined. The emissions of the super-rich 1 percent during 2019 were enough to cause 1.3 million deaths due to heat.[23] The damage done by the 1 percent is compounded by the fact that their wealth is heavily invested in fossil fuel companies, and they use their influence in politics and the media to promote the continuation of government subsidies to fossil fuel industries. Beyond the richest 1 percent, the richest 10 percent are also key to the climate story,

---

20. Keum, *Together Towards Life*, §23.
21. "Arusha Conference Report," 11.
22. New Economics Foundation, cited in McKibben, *Deep Economy*, 196.
23. Oxfam, *Climate Equality*, x.

together emitting approximately half of all global emissions.[24] This powerful group has used its influence to achieve the criminalization of environmental protest in many parts of the world, provoking George Monbiot to observe that "those who seek to protect the living planet by democratic means are arrested en masse and imprisoned by the authorities, while the people and organisations trashing our life-support systems are untouched by the law."[25]

In her foreword to the Oxfam report, Swedish climate activist Greta Thunberg translates its technical language into straight talk: "Climate breakdown and inequality are linked together and fuel each other. If we are to overcome one, we must overcome both.... This report reveals a perverse reality: those who have done the least to cause the climate crisis are the ones who are suffering the most. And those who have done the most will likely suffer the least."[26] She takes the super-rich 1 percent to task, pointing out that "they have stolen our planet's resources to fuel their lavish lifestyles. A short trip on a private jet will produce more carbon than the average person emits all year. They are sacrificing us at the altar of their greed."[27] While the richest can insulate themselves from adverse effects of climate change by protecting their multiple, air-conditioned homes, it is the most vulnerable who are heavily hit by drought, flooding, and relentless heat.

The scandal that particularly outrages Thunberg is that "the people most responsible for the climate crisis—mainly white, privileged men—are also the ones who have been given a leading role in getting us out of it.... How have we left the culprits in charge when there is so much at stake? Why are they in charge when time and again they have shown us that they prioritize their greed and short-term economic profits above people and planet? Is it any wonder progress is so slow?"[28]

There has long been an awareness that the legacy of the slave trade and European colonial rule over large parts of the globe has created grave economic inequality. Climate science now reveals that emissions from the industries that drove European colonial expansion built up an excess of atmospheric carbon. The prosperity of the West was built on grabbing far more than its fair share of the atmospheric space available to absorb

---

24. Oxfam, *Climate Equality*, xv.
25. Monbiot, "Here's a Question COP28 Won't Address."
26. Thunberg, "Foreword," vi.
27. Thunberg, "Foreword," vi.
28. Thunberg, "Foreword," vi–vii.

carbon before it starts to do damage. The injustice at the heart of the global economy is even greater than has been understood before. The amount of carbon emissions that the atmosphere can absorb safely is finite and the West built its prosperity by using up most of the available space. It therefore carries a great moral responsibility to act justly towards those who meet climate change from a disadvantaged position and who are most vulnerable to its effects. There is an urgency to this. As Mary Ann Sering, climate change secretary for the Philippines, told the 2013 UN climate summit in Warsaw, "I am beginning to feel like we are negotiating who is to live and who is to die."[29]

The inequality highlighted in the Oxfam report is not only obscene at a human level but is remorselessly bringing about a climate catastrophe that threatens the future of life on earth. The onus falls on the wealthy and powerful to look beyond their own short-term interests and use their privileged position to work to secure our common future. As political economist Geoff Mann explains: "We are in desperate need of a politics that looks catastrophic uncertainty square in the face. That would mean taking much bigger and more transformative steps: all but eliminating fossil fuels, for a start, and prioritizing democratic institutions over markets. The burden of this effort must fall almost entirely on the richest people and richest parts of the world, because it is they who continue to gamble with everyone's else's fate."[30] In *Laudate Deum* Pope Francis poses a question to the powerful: "What would induce anyone, at this stage, to hold on to power, only to be remembered for their inability to take action when it was urgent and necessary to do so?"[31] Greta Thunberg's question is even more blunt: "We are at the beginning of a mass extinction and all you can talk about is money and fairy tales of endless economic growth. How dare you!"[32]

ECUMENICAL VISION INSPIRING ACTION

"Fundamentally," suggests author and social activist Naomi Klein, "the task is to articulate not just an alternative set of policy proposals but an alternative worldview to rival the one at the heart of the ecological crisis—embedded in interdependence rather than hyper-individualism, reciprocity

---

29. Cited in Klein, *This Changes Everything*, 276.
30. Mann, "Treading Thin Air," 19.
31. Pope Francis, *Laudate Deum*, §60.
32. Thunberg, in Oxfam, *Climate Equality*, 3.

rather than dominance, and cooperation rather than hierarchy."[33] These notes are very reminiscent of those that have been struck by the ecumenical movement during its hundred-year history. While it sprang from concern to build relationships of cooperation and unity among churches and missions, it always had a broader horizon. Its vision extended to the whole inhabited earth. No one and no issue could be excluded from its concern. Its instinct has always been about breaking down barriers, strengthening understanding, pooling resources, and building community. The challenge and the opportunity today are to break new ground by bringing this ecumenical experience to bear on the entire fabric of the natural order, especially the relationship between humanity and the non-human creation in all its diversity.

At the core of the ecumenical vision is a sense of common belonging that stretches across space and time. Today this needs to be brought to bear on the ecological crisis. Ecological theologian Ernst Conradie notes that "while Christians in some contexts contribute disproportionally to carbon emissions, Christians in other contexts are or will increasingly become the victims of climate change." This is a test of ecumenical accountability. "Clearly," states Conradie, "the quality of fellowship between churches provides a test case for the credibility of their witness to the mission of the triune God in the world."[34] Pope Francis looks across time to observe, "Today's ecological crisis, especially climate change, threatens the very future of the human family. Future generations stand to inherit a greatly spoiled world. Our children and grandchildren should not have to pay the cost of our generation's irresponsibility."[35] To put the matter more positively, the climate crisis supplies an opportunity to demonstrate that we belong together. As the Catholic Bishops of the United States have affirmed, "Our care for one another and our care for the earth are intimately bound together."[36]

If the ecological crisis is to be met with any hope of success, it is very clear today that the human community will need unity, it will need mission, and it will need movement. Here the ecumenical movement brings relevant experience. When the modern missionary movement was inspired by its passion for worldwide evangelism, its leaders were impressed by how much more effective it could be if its divisions and fragmentation could

---

33. Klein, *This Changes Everything*, 462.
34. Conradie, "Environment," 330.
35. Cited in Frankopan, *Earth Transformed*, 4.
36. Cited in Pope Francis, *Laudate Deum*, §3.

be replaced by cooperation and unity. In particular, the International Missionary Council from its foundation in 1921 was greatly concerned about achieving just relationships and mutual respect between the Western missions who were its first members and the non-Western churches that were then just emerging in a colonial world with a great imbalance of power.[37]

Today's ecological crisis calls for a similar kind of movement—one that brings together a diversity of actors to confront a massive challenge and to form just relationships between the powerful and the marginalized. Today's crisis will require those involved to be "ecumenical to the maximum," creating as big a tent as possible and building a widely inclusive movement that spans many different nations, faiths, and identities. After all, the earth itself is at stake. We know from history that a religious vision can unify and motivate people like little else. Now the challenge is to cast a vision that is inspirational not only for one faith community but for all. Sometimes different religious communities have struggled to find common ground—now it is literally beneath their feet. Scientific research has been essential in getting to the bottom of the causes of climate change and demonstrating what the solutions might be. But this knowledge in itself proves to be insufficient to ignite a movement with enough power to fundamentally change the status quo. In its time, the missionary movement endowed people with extraordinary motivation, and their work was transformative in many places. Could the same dynamic be created for the new mission that is needed today: the mission to reshape human life and behavior in such a way that the earth can be sustained and cherished?

---

37. See Barreto, "International Missionary Council."

3

The Economy We Need to Create

Michael: We have been hearing a lot about the global cost of living crisis. You are living in Malawi—is it affecting people there?

Kenneth: Very much so. Malawi had to devalue its currency by 40 percent in late 2023. This has led to price hikes that have put even basic commodities out of reach for the many people who are living on less than a dollar a day.

Michael: How are people responding to these harsh conditions?

Kenneth: I always marvel at the resilience and community solidarity that enables Malawians to survive and flourish even in face of great adversity. But I worry now that this is being stretched too far and that it will reach a breaking point.

Michael: What about young people growing up in this situation? How are they looking at things?

Kenneth: Malawi has an average age of nineteen so there are many young people coming through the education system with great hopes. But all too often their hopes are dashed by lack of opportunity. Through the internet they can see how people elsewhere live prosperous lives, which highlights how bleak their prospects are.

Michael: Is everyone in Malawi facing such deprivation?

Kenneth: No, there is a small elite that is very comfortably off, people who often have connections to government or sources of income outside the country. The problem is that this small group seem to have more and more while the majority have less and less.

Michael: It all sounds very discouraging. What could change things for the better?

Kenneth: There needs to be a different kind of society—one that is affirmative of everyone; and there needs to be a different kind of economy—one that is inclusive and that can offer genuine hope. This will not be achieved without a movement for change in Malawi, nor without a movement for change in the world as a whole.

THE EARLY YEARS OF the twenty-first century have been turbulent ones for the human community. For many around the world today conditions are volatile, conflictive, discouraging, and deteriorating. The majority find themselves faced with a hyper-complex constellation of interlocking issues that make their life ever more intolerable: poverty, unemployment, reduction of social welfare, depletion of land, a more hostile climate, war and conflict, disease and suffering, gender injustice, exclusion, and marginalization. While there are islands of prosperity that are well protected from such adversities, in most situations, vulnerability is increasing. Many lives have been cut short, many have suffered traumatic violence including rape, and many have had to flee their homes and face the privation and uncertainty of life as a refugee. Such tragic developments are not occurring by accident or by some unexplained misfortune. It becomes increasingly apparent that they are the result of a merciless economic system that has been imposed on the global community. It employs a rhetoric that promises growth, prosperity, and happiness but, in reality, these turn out to be the preserve of a powerful elite, while it is a very different story for the majority.

An economy that brings lavish rewards to 1 percent and fails to address the needs and aspirations of 99 percent is now at a crisis point. It cannot continue on the current trajectory. The Blue Planet Prize laureates presented a stark conclusion: "In face of an absolutely unprecedented emergency, society has no choice but to take dramatic action to avert a collapse of civilization. Either we will change our ways and build an entirely new kind of global society, or they will be changed for us."[1] Such is the magnitude of the crisis we face today that gradual and incremental adjustments are unlikely to resolve it. A radical reconfiguration of the human community and the way it lives on earth is called for.

---

1. Cited in Klein, *This Changes Everything*, 22.

THE ECONOMY WE NEED TO CREATE

FAILURE OF THE ECONOMY

This situation has not come about because no one had been paying attention to the economy. On the contrary, it is a constant focus of attention as governments and businesses pursue the holy grail of high rates of economic growth. The problem, however, is that when statistics celebrating economic growth are published, these run counter to the experience of most people who are finding that the resources at their disposal are becoming fewer and the task of sustaining life for themselves and their families is becoming harder. It becomes clear that the much-vaunted economic growth is not equitable in its effects.

It has become apparent that the prevailing economic system is systematically distributing resources so that a wealthy minority becomes even more wealthy while the majority become ever more impoverished. Noam Chomsky notes a revealing brochure prepared by the Citigroup bank for potential investors in which "the bank's analysts describe a world that is divided into two blocs, the plutonomy and the rest, creating a global society in which growth is powered by the wealthy few and largely consumed by them. Left out of the gains of the plutonomy are the 'non-rich,' the vast majority, now sometimes called the 'global precariat,' the workforce living an unstable and increasingly penurious existence."[2] The system seems to have no corrective mechanism, so it is simply going from bad to worse.

One reason that this inequitable and divisive system continues to prevail is that it is underpinned by an ideology that has developed immense power. Proponents of the neoliberal economic system endow it with ultimacy, explaining it in quasi-religious terms. Political scientist Francis Fukuyama, for example, declared that "it is definitely proved that with the collapse of the socialist bloc, the capitalist market system is the apex of the evolution of human history and we are about the enter the 'Promised Land.'"[3] The market is accorded such an absolute authority that it is beyond challenge. Even when its effects are obviously unjust and harmful, there can be no questioning. As Latin American theologian Jung Mo Sung has written, "When one believes and has faith that all desires can be satisfied with the limitless accumulation of wealth made possible by technical progress, one also believes that the social system that generates maximum technological progress is the true way to 'paradise,' to 'abundant life.' To the

---

2. Chomsky, *Who Rules the World?*, 65.

3. Cited in Sung, *Desire, Market and Religion*, 13.

extent that one believes that the capitalist market system is this unique way, without any alternative, all is justified and legitimized in the name of the market. The market system is seen as the 'way and the truth' which leads us to abundant life."[4]

Granting supreme authority to the market has created not only an economic system but also a supporting culture which is highly pervasive in today's world. There has been a commodification of the whole of life, governing our understanding of the natural world and even of ourselves. As the WCC Arusha Conference noted: "The culture of money seeks to define and dominate every aspect of human activity and every creature of God's world. It forms possessor-consumers to be compliant constituents of an economically constructed world."[5] Market forces are accorded a God-like authority as they become the absolute around which everything must revolve. Little wonder that critics look on the claims of neoliberalism as a matter of idolatry. Treating the market as God has a knock-on effect on how we understand our humanity. When an ecumenical conference was convened at São Paulo in 2012, it concluded: "There is a distorted definition of anthropology in neoliberalism in which human beings are defined by financial and economic value and not by their intrinsic dignity as persons created in the image of God. This anthropology has nested in humanity, colonizing our mind and our dreams."[6] The neoliberal model has been immensely successful in extending its influence around the world. The problem is that the results of its application have been disastrous—both for the natural environment and for the human community.

The climate activist Bill McKibben has a very simple way of explaining the situation: "For most of human history, the two birds More and Better roosted on the same branch. You could toss one stone and hope to hit them both. . . . But the distinguishing feature of our moment is this: Better has flown a few trees over to make her nest. That changes everything. Now, if you've got the stone of your own life, or your own society, gripped in your hand, you have to choose between them. It's More *or* Better."[7] This means that economic growth is not the criterion of human happiness. McKibben acknowledges that for the very poor, having more will make their life better. But for those who are comfortable, acquiring even more will not make their

---

4. Sung, *Desire, Market and Religion*, 17.
5. "Arusha Conference Report," 16.
6. *São Paulo Statement*.
7. McKibben, *Deep Economy*, 1.

life better. Research in his own country, the USA, revealed that, "All in all, we have more stuff and less happiness."[8]

Endless extraction and overconsumption turn out not to be an economic model that makes for human fulfillment. The neoliberal system is not even working well for those who profit from it. Much less for the many who are losing out as the system sucks resources towards its powerful centers. Jung Mo Sung asks what the suffering of the majority means from the perspective of Christian faith and what "the Christian faith can bring to the struggle against the 'empire'?"[9]

The 2012 São Paulo ecumenical conference attempted an answer to this question: "We are called to find a new and just international financial architecture oriented towards satisfying the needs of people and the realisation of all economic, social and cultural rights and human dignity. Such architecture must be focused on reducing the intolerable chasm between the rich and the poor and on preventing ecological destruction. This requires a system which does not serve greed but which embraces alternative economies that foster a spirituality of enough and a lifestyle of simplicity, solidarity, social inclusion and justice."[10]

This is not to say that there is no place for the market. It is to recognize, however, that leaving everything to market forces is a recipe for injustice, exclusion, and ecological catastrophe. A 2023 Oxfam report draws the distinction: "Markets are a vital engine of growth and prosperity, but we must no longer accept the faulty premise that the engine should steer the car. The idea that the wellbeing of all and the survival of our planet can only be created as a by-product of the pursuit of financial profit and ever-greater wealth for the few must be fundamentally rejected."[11]

This in turn raises the question of who is going to drive the car? The Oxfam report has an answer: "People should be put back in charge of their destiny, and democratically elected governments, not corporates, should shape our economy. Our economies should be purposively redesigned and reimagined with a primary focus on the twin goals of human and planetary flourishing."[12] Likewise, when the São Paulo ecumenical conference proposed a drastic overhaul of the world economy and international financial

---

8. McKibben, *Deep Economy*, 36.
9. Sung, *Desire, Market and Religion*, 22.
10. *São Paulo Statement*.
11. Oxfam, *Climate Equality*, xxviii.
12. Oxfam, *Climate Equality*, xii.

system, it recognized that a crucial step would be for the financial markets and the economy to be brought under the primacy of democratic decision-making structures. This would allow financial markets to "function as good servants rather than bad masters in political and economic life. Economics has to be embedded in social, ecological and political life rather than the other way around."[13] This, however, poses the question as to how well our political structures today are equipped to enact such a fundamental reform of the working of the global economy?

FAILURE OF POLITICS

In order to achieve the kind of reimagining and reconstruction of the global economy that is urgently called for today, there is need for innovative, united, and reforming political action on an unprecedented scale. Unfortunately, just at the moment when it needs to raise its game like never before, the political system seems to have been evacuated of its integrity and purpose. While this configures differently in different countries, there is a clearly discernible pattern that is consistent across the globe. When the all-powerful idea guiding human affairs is the supremacy of the market, the options available to political actors are drastically reduced. Their role becomes the subservient one of removing any national obstacles that might be impeding the effective operation of the global market. Such wealth and power are concentrated in the hands of those at the helm of large corporations that they can exercise financial muscle to make sure that politicians serve their interests.

Nnimmo Bassey, chair of Friends of the Earth International, is gloomy about the situation: "Politics today has been reduced to a lucrative venture where one looks out mainly for returns on investment rather than on what one can contribute to rebuild highly degraded environments, communities, and a nation."[14] Even progressive political parties with a history of working for economic justice and social inclusion seem to have been sucked into the vortex created by the supremacy of market forces. George Monbiot reaches the damning conclusion that "winning, they came to believe, required the renunciation of almost everything they had stood for, and its replacement with the ideology of their opponents. Only when their politics became acceptable to the proprietors of the newspapers and other billionaires, they

---

13. *São Paulo Statement*.
14. Bassey, *To Cook a Continent*, cited in Chomsky, *Who Rules the World?*, 97.

believed, was electoral success possible. To win, they had to lose. Taking power meant abandoning power; victory required retreat on all fronts."[15] Thus the force of neoliberalism carries all before it. "Most mainstream parties," notes Monbiot, "seek only to tweak the existing narratives. This is why they seem effete, passionless and exhausted."[16]

What then is politics about today? Many have concluded that it is not anything with which it is worth becoming involved. It appears to be nothing more than an elite political class jostling for position as they seek to feather their own nests. As Yascha Mounk has noted: "Citizens have long been disillusioned with politics; now they have grown restless, angry, even disdainful. Party systems have long seemed frozen; now, authoritarian populists are on the rise around the world. . . . Voters have long disliked particular parties, politicians, or governments; now, many of them have become fed up with liberal democracy itself."[17] Popular withdrawal and disengagement from conventional politics is now a defining social trend. Hence political scientist Peter Mair observes, "The age of party democracy has passed. . . . Parties are failing . . . as a result of a process of mutual withdrawal or abandonment, whereby citizens retreat into private life or into more specialized and often ad hoc forms of representation, while the party leaderships retreat into the institutions, drawing their terms of reference ever more readily from their roles as governors or public-office holders."[18] Mair's research demonstrates that there is less electoral participation, greater electoral volatility, reduced party loyalties, falling party membership—and that these trends are consistent in every part of Europe.[19]

The result is that "there is a world of the citizens—or a host of particular worlds of the citizens—and a world of the politicians and parties, and the interaction between them steadily diminishes. Citizens change from participants into spectators, while the elites win more and more space in which to pursue their own particular interests. The result is the beginning of a new form of democracy, one in which the citizens stay at home while the parties get on with governing."[20] This creates a perfect environment for politicians to dance to the tune of big business, with very limited accountability to

---

15. Monbiot, *Out of the Wreckage*, 165.
16. Monbiot, *Out of the Wreckage*, 6.
17. Cited in Mills et al., *Democracy Works*, 5.
18. Mair, *Ruling the Void*, 16.
19. Mair, *Ruling the Void*, 17–44.
20. Mair, *Ruling the Void*, 98.

the wider society. It might seem surprising that their increasingly impoverished voters would tolerate such a situation but there are formidable forces at play that keep them in their place. "As long as the general population is passive, apathetic, and diverted to consumerism or hatred of the vulnerable," observes Chomsky, "then the powerful can do as they please, and those who survive will be left to contemplate the outcome."[21]

BUILDING ALTERNATIVE VISION

The grip of neoliberalism on the human community is expressed by a phrase often attributed to the British Prime Minister Margaret Thatcher: "there is no alternative." This conviction is one that faith communities are well equipped to contest as they experience the divisive and destructive impact of this prevailing economic model. The resources of their faith equip them to contest Thatcher's assertion and advocate an alternative vision of the human community, one that stands in sharp contrast to the pervasive neoliberal reality.

An alternative story of hope and transformation is needed. In the case of Christianity, the faith is built on belief in a reality that stands in contrast to the prevailing plausibility structure. The Christian faith began during the time of the Roman Empire when a dominant military and political power attempted to impose its beliefs and values on the entire Mediterranean world. The first Christians were people who saw things differently because they took their bearings from the life, teaching, death, and resurrection of Jesus of Nazareth. In a world where everyone was under immense pressure to confess that "Caesar is Lord," they defiantly took a different line—"Jesus is Lord." This was an affront to the power of the empire and from time to time it took steps to crush the dissidents. In the famous words of Tertullian, however, the blood of the martyrs became the seed of the church. Christianity spread and grew until even the empire had to accept it. Finally, the empire would decline and fall while Christianity went on to grow and flourish. This memory is relevant today as people of faith engage with a dominant ideology that is supported by massive economic and military power.

One device that enabled Christianity in its early days to challenge a prevailing consensus is apocalyptic literature, exemplified by the book of Revelation as well as other passages in the New Testament. As Duncan

21. Chomsky, *Who Rules the World?*, 56.

Forrester explains: "Apocalyptic denies the finality and acceptability of the existing order of things. . . . The pretensions of rulers and dominant authorities are cut down to size and relativized. Apocalyptic declares that the existing powers are not the final manifestation of God's purposes; their days are numbered."[22] This demonstrates the subversive power of Christian faith. It exposed and denounced the idolatry of the Roman Empire, the arrogance of power and wealth. Powers and authorities that look as if they are set to dominate forever can be exposed as false and time-limited.

Not only are their pretensions demolished but an utterly contrasting vision of the nature of human life and destiny is advanced. As Forrester continues, "An alternative order, in which the faithful, the weak and the excluded will have an honoured place, is not only possible, but it is promised and will break in and disrupt the existing order. Apocalyptic thus nourishes a confident hope not only that things *can* be different, but that they *will* be different, for, if believers are faithful, God will bring out of the present disorder a new era which will be characterised by peace and justice and the vindication of the oppressed."[23]

With their eschatological imagination, the churches are uniquely well placed to advance the conviction that "another world is possible." Such advocacy requires the churches to articulate a convincing vision of what a better future can look like. But this is more than just an exercise in conjecture. It needs to be lived out in practical reality. The Christian leaders who gathered at Arusha in 2018 for the WCC World Mission Conference reached the conclusion that "we must engage in a determined attempt to present, for this generation, a faithful alternative to the spiritual formation offered by the culture of money. This calls not only for prophetic critique but for practical, local action to build an alternative economy, one that is just and sustainable."[24] This will never be easy since it is a matter of swimming against the tide and resisting the formidable forces that drive the current structures. It will require the formation of communities of Christians that are resilient in the face of injustice, that are humble and courageous in persistently challenging the unjust system. When others flag or become disillusioned by apparently immovable resistance to positive change, the churches are energized by faith in the promise that the purpose of God

---

22. Forrester, *Apocalypse Now?*, 59.
23. Forrester, *Apocalypse Now?*, 59.
24. "Arusha Conference Report," 16.

revealed in Jesus Christ will ultimately find expression in the new world which God will bring to birth.

It might look like a matter of David versus Goliath but, just as David brought his sling to the battle, so churches have resources to offer that might turn out to be more powerful than they first appear to be. Throughout history they have demonstrated their ability to mobilize people around a common faith and purpose. They can instill motivation, vision, fellowship, solidarity. The challenge today might be to do this not in any exclusive way but in an inviting, inclusive way, building a broader coalition. As Njoki Njehu, Pan-Africa regional coordinator for Fight Inequality Alliance, has written, "We must build peoples' movements bigger than we have ever known. Climate warriors and inequality fighters; rural farmers and feminists; trade unionists and youth activists must join arms across the planet to scream 'Enough! No More!' We must build an unstoppable force, coming together to fight and win a radically more equal world, where everyone can live in dignity, and our planet is restored and renewed for all future generations."[25]

TENDING THE WOUNDS

Such a transformation is very unlikely to be effected by today's political elites. Therefore, the force to effect change needs to come from the bottom up. Here the churches with their vast networks of grassroots communities can be key players, not acting alone but making common cause with all who are determined to confront death-dealing systems and construct an economy of life. Many of the most marginalized people in today's world find meaning and hope through their faith and participation in church life. Their discipleship can become a key resource, inspiring action for justice and building collaboration among the dispossessed.

With their prophetic calling, it can be expected that churches in today's world will make common cause with others who are resisting neoliberal domination. In terms of analysis and advocacy they can find a great deal in common with other faith communities and with those who pursue justice from a non-religious standpoint. Churches must enter such collaboration humbly, recognizing that they have been to varying degrees complicit in the system that they are now resisting. Tinyiko Maluleke has pointed out how churches in South Africa were implicated in the system of apartheid,

---

25. Njehu, "Foreword," viii.

yet they also managed to offer an alternative vision of society and to play a leading role in resisting and overcoming apartheid. If they were able to play a part in healing a broken nation, they had to recognize that they were "wounded healers."[26]

At their best the churches can bring a certain distinctive quality to the shared struggle in that their prophetic role is intertwined with their pastoral calling. This was well illustrated in one of the world's most troubled countries—South Sudan. After visiting in 2010, Nicholas Kristof wrote in the *New York Times*: "I came here to impoverished southern Sudan to write about Sudanese problems, not the . . . Church's. Yet once again, I am awed that so many of the selfless people serving the world's neediest are lowly nuns and priests."[27] This is not something that happens just by accident. It rests on deep theological foundations, as John Ashworth and others indicate: "Unlike most NGOs and indeed most of the international community, the Church is in it for the long haul. The Church embodies immense patience and looks beyond the present suffering to a hope-filled future. In the Christian archetype death comes before resurrection, but in the end, resurrection does come."[28]

This resurrection hope plays a very practical role in situations where great injustice prevails and efforts to challenge it are continuously thwarted. The strongest protesters, the most fearless advocates can be worn down, discouraged and defeated when they seem to be getting nowhere and they are being crushed by the might of the powerful forces that they hoped to challenge. Here the faith perspective can make all the difference. As Duncan Forrester explains: "The saints leave vengeance to God; their task is to demonstrate the power of powerlessness, 'strength made perfect in weakness.'"[29] Christians are equipped to remain resilient and to persevere against all the odds. Their faith gives them the conviction that, in the words of Alan Lewis, "trust, defencelessness, and vulnerability are in themselves, despite all appearances, finally more productive and protective than all stratagems for aggression or defence, attack or retaliation, self-assertion or self-protection."[30] This counterintuitive confidence sustains Christians for the long haul that lies ahead of them if they are to challenge and transform

---

26. Maluleke, "Wounded Healers in the Service of the Wounded," 140–41.
27. Cited in Ashworth et al., *Voice of the Voiceless*, 13.
28. Ashworth et al., *Voice of the Voiceless*, 164.
29. Forrester, *Apocalypse Now?*, 62.
30. Lewis, *Between Cross and Resurrection*, 321.

the world order that prevails today. As Martin Luther King Jr. put it: "Returning violence for violence multiplies violence, adding deeper darkness to a night already devoid of stars. Darkness cannot drive out darkness; only light can do that. Hate cannot drive out hate; only love can do that."[31]

To adopt such a posture is to run a high risk of being hurt. Identifying with the vulnerable and the marginalized involves sharing their lot. It is a violent world, and taking sides with the victimized exposes us to the risk of becoming wounded as they are.[32] This prompted Robert Schreiter to suggest that "a response to living within the *Missio Dei* today" is to engage in a *"missio ad vulnera,* or a mission to the wounds."[33] Perhaps it is the same awareness that caused Pope Francis in 2013, at the beginning of his pontificate, to imagine the church as a field hospital: "I see clearly ... that the thing the church needs most today is the ability to heal wounds and to warm the hearts of the faithful; it needs nearness, proximity. I see the church as a field hospital after battle. It is useless to ask a seriously injured person if he has high cholesterol and about the level of his blood sugar. You have to heal his wounds. Then we can talk about everything else. Heal the wounds, heal the wounds. . . . And you have to start from the ground up."[34]

Combining the roles of prophet, pastor, and physician might be what will lend a distinctive quality to the role of the churches in the task of transformation in which they must now play their part. So complete is the capture of state organs and media outlets by the global neoliberal economic system that it will take something extraordinary to dislodge it. Yet this is what must be achieved if the natural environment is to be sustained and livable human life is to be made possible. Now is the time for Christians to join hands with many others, ready to receive their insights while offering the gifts of alternative vision inspired by biblical apocalyptic and distinctive discipleship shaped by death and resurrection. Then they can form an ecumenical movement with the breadth, vision, and tenacity that will be needed to transform today's death-dealing dynamics into an economy of life.

---

31. Cited in Forrester, *Apocalypse Now?*, 88.
32. See Kollman, "Urgent Demands of the Present."
33. Cited in Bevans, "'Your Light Must Shine before Others,'" 159.
34. Cited in Bevans, "'Your Light Must Shine before Others,'" 159–60.

4

The Development We Need to Empower

Michael: Marina, how is it that you proposed and promoted the inclusion of a chapter on development in our book?

Marina: In Mizoram, my home state in Northeast India, education came with mission and the churches continue to offer education and health care for all. In mainland India churches also continue to provide education and health care, running some of the most respected schools and hospitals.

Michael: Is there any problem with that?

Marina: For the churches the question is how to negotiate their offers in a context where good or excellent services are expensive and thus exclusive for many. On the other hand, Christians are accused of luring people by these services into their fold, thus alienating them from their original identity which is claimed to be Hindu.

Michael: Is there a way out of this impasse?

Marina: I think there is something to learn if we look back into how the discourses on mission and development were constructed. The accusations mentioned point to the risky and open process in which mission finds itself in many regions. Giving up such services offered to all would leave mission with proclamation and this would confirm the suspicion that Christians cannot do other than convert. The solution in this crisis should be sought in the emphasis that life in abundance is God's mission for all. Mission is joining in working for justice for all, in cooperation with people of other faiths and without restricting life in abundance to those who become Christians. As Christians we can witness to our God by living in solidarity with our neighbors.

MISSION AND SERVICE

IT IS A COMMONPLACE in the history of missions that mission to the so-called non-Christian world (Edinburgh 1910) came as a "trinity": inviting to faith, educating, and healing. Educating was based on the assumption that it would be salvific (salutary) for the so-called "heathen" to be able to read the Bible.[1] Bible translation and the desire to distribute the Bible led to the establishment of Bible societies with growing expertise in translating the Bible into the vernacular languages. The teaching of reading and writing led to the establishment of schools. They expanded their curriculum beyond the Bible to include more subjects. Education then began to promote the concept of developing indigenous church leadership.[2] Health care began with attempts to provide for the missionaries' self-care as well as their being able to improve the situation of the people by providing medical services and combating disease.[3] This resulted in the establishment of health stations, hospitals, and then medical schools to train indigenous persons to take over this role and responsibility.

Development was clearly on the agenda of the missionary societies even when the conceptual language was not present. The importance of these efforts for mission is evident by the gradual professionalization of the services which best can be seen in health care which led to the establishment of medical missions. They moved from basic medical training for missionaries (and their wives) to medical personnel who, in turn, now needed missional training.[4]

One effect of the professionalization was that the practice of mission diversified into different branches and disciplines, each with its own methodology and practical implementation, influenced by secular disciplines.[5]

---

1. *Education in Relation to the Christianisation of National Life.*

2. *Church in the Mission Field*, ch. 5. "Training and Employment of Workers," 171–206; particularly on "Theological Training," 182–88.

3. "Minutes of the Sectional Meeting of Medical Delegates, etc., held at the World Missionary Conference 1910," in *Preparation of Missionaries*, 289–90.

4. "It is given to him to represent directly that large and clearly most important side of our Lord's earthly ministry, which was spent in 'doing good' and 'healing all manner of sickness and all manner of disease among the people.'" *Preparation of Missionaries*, "The Application of These Principles to the Training of Medical Missionaries and Nurses," 134–45, at 137.

5. "That the professional preparation of Medical Missionaries should be as thorough as possible, that no one who has not passed through the complete medical curriculum and obtained a diploma or degree in Medicine from a recognised examining body, should

This led to the diversification of the mission movements and later to the employment of specialists, for example in agriculture or in the training of manual workers, to support mission in general. One of the challenges for mission was therefore, how to understand theologically the intrinsic unity of these different branches of mission as proclamation and as acts of compassion to improve living conditions.

This progression led to the establishment of Christian development agencies such as World Vision (1950), Tearfund (1971), MICAH global (1999) in the Evangelical world and Action by Churches Together (Act) International (1995) in the context of the World Council of Churches (WCC) and Lutheran World Federation–related churches. It was felt that there was a need to coordinate the activities of faith-based organizations in development especially gearing towards sustainability. In 2010, the Action by Churches Together (ACT) Alliance was launched, becoming the largest coalition of Protestant and Orthodox faith-based actors working on humanitarian, developmental, and advocacy issues with more than 140 members in 120 countries.[6]

All such organizations struggle with their self-understanding of being in God's mission but not to confuse actual aid with evangelism, lest they be accused of working for conversion or worse, not helping the body but manipulating the minds.[7] The fact that in some Northern European countries the organizations are able in part to use funds from government development budgets shows that they are successful in mastering this balance in the eyes of the back donors. This also hints to the fact that in the public space development aid is an accepted form of the "mission" of these societies to the rest of the world. The professionalization of development work, its detachment from mission and the growing number of secular development agencies or NGOs seem, on the other hand, to have left to mission only the message of salvation. What both continue to share is the criticism received that they reflect a Western sense of superiority and universalism.

How does one cope with the tension between the motivation for mission and development without using development for conversion? Does the differentiation between mission and development have a negative feedback

---

assume the title of Medical Missionary." "That those Missionaries who are compelled to live in districts where there are no 'Medical Missionaries,' and where no qualified medical or surgical assistance is available, should have that knowledge which shall enable them to treat minor ailments and accidents." *Preparation of Missionaries*, 289–90.

6. https://actalliance.org/who-we-are/.

7. See *Called to Transformation*, 50–51.

effect on the image of mission? We will explore these questions by sketching the course of the development and mission discourses in broad strokes and conclude with some remarks on mission.

DEVELOPMENT DISCOURSES

President Truman's inaugural address in 1949 is seen by many as the introduction of the idea that the richer nations have an obligation to support developing countries.[8] Truman situated this idea clearly within the fight of the post-war bloc systems, accusing communism of being able to solve social problems and conflicts only by oppression and violence. To counter this perceived threat to the "free world," he called on the democratic countries: "Our aim should be to help the free peoples of the world, through their own efforts, to produce more food, more clothing, more materials for housing, and more mechanical power to lighten their burdens."[9]

Development was thus presented as the instrument of the free world's mission to ensure a peaceful progress of poorer nations, and to make them less susceptible to communist or socialist ideologies by educating them in democracy. The concept developed through the period of independence of emerging nations and of formal decolonization into the era of globalization. Inspired by the term "Third World," introduced by the French scholar Alfred Sauvy in 1952, the capitalist countries were called the "First World," those of the Communist bloc the "Second World." Underdevelopment was the perceived common denominator of the various countries grouped together as the "Third World." The people in these countries expected far-reaching social and political change, and their elites hoped for economic progress, modernization, sustainable development, education, and health systems.[10] In this turbulent period the bloc states competed over which ideology would persuade the countries clubbed under "Third World" to accept the development the competing nations were envisioning for them. There was a strong secular but missionary motivation in the First World countries' attempt to sketch out the path of development for the developing countries. The mission at that time was to use the instrument of

---

8. Clarke and Donnelly, "Learning from Missionaries," 169.
9. Truman, "Inaugural Address, January 20, 1949."
10. Behera, "'Global North and Global South,'" 31–32.

development to prevent communist or socialist revolutions in the countries concerned.[11]

From the 1980s onwards, the rights-based approach became an important framework for development. The focus shifted from relief and welfare and from large-scale programs to alleviate poverty and develop economic progress to the mission to empower communities and to promote social justice and human rights.[12] In that era, religious beliefs were seen by many modernists as the cause of alleged backwardness and economic underdevelopment. It seems that these critics considered religion as strong force when it promoted fundamentalist and violent politics, and as soft where it seems to chime in with liberal or progressive values.

In the 2000s the World Bank initiated a discussion on the role of religion in development, focusing on faith-based organizations, for example, religious communities, as actors in development processes.[13] Michael Biehl argues that this was a move away from the prevailing modernist view in the last decades of the twentieth century that religion would disappear with the progress of economics, science, and human rights in the developing world. One of the strengths of faith-based organizations which now was seen as conducive for development was that they could approach their locally rooted communities which existed before development projects started and remained after they ended. Another strength seen was that religious communities are transnational actors, connecting across borders and continents and at the same time local and indigenous organizations.[14] In African countries, for example, religion is an important factor for development and religious communities such as churches are heavily involved in such activities.[15]

MISSION DISCOURSE

The debate on development among the mission organizations is older.[16] There is a long tradition of mission discourse on service, be it on *diaconia*

---

11. Biehl, "Religion, Development and Mission," 103.
12. Clarke and Donnelly, "Learning from Missionaries," 172–73.
13. See Biehl, "Religion, Development and Mission," 107.
14. Biehl, "Religion, Development and Mission," 107.
15. Gunda, "Rethinking Development in Africa and the Role of Religion," 55, 78.
16. See also Drønen, "Christian Mission and International Development."

or on development.[17] In the nineteenth century and the first decades of the twentieth century, efforts to professionalize the services were fed by the sense of Western superiority that was particularly evident in the fields of medical knowledge and practice. An observation on the mental attitude in the decades after 1850 illustrates this, stating that medicine was a field in which the supremacy of the "white" was so obvious that the practices of other cultures or indigenous knowledge were ruled out. "The new mission clinic was not, however, to be the exclusive preserve of the secular medic; it was to be a hybrid in which the priest and the doctor worked side-by-side, one preaching while the other healed."[18]

In the long run, the growing professionalization worked in favor of a bifurcation of mission and development, even where the churches were involved. The different branches of mission had improved the knowledge available in the West, for example on tropical diseases, anthropology, language studies. Missionaries thus supported the development of the secular disciplines which in the long run led to a secularizing tendency in the services provided by the missions. In the period of independence and formal decolonization, schools and medical institutions in many countries were handed over to the emerging nation-states. There was a growing belief that it was modern for churches to disengage from such activities and to hand over to the emerging nation-states. It was, however, discovered that in many countries health care became an income-generating commodity, making it inaccessible to the poor. Similar observations can be made in the field of education. In contexts in which good and excellent services have to be paid for, the challenge for the churches is how to maintain open access for people with lower income or from marginalized groups.

In the debates about mission and development awareness grew that the motivation for such activities was Christian, but the knowledge used was that of secular disciplines. There also was a growing awareness that caring for people's lives and livelihoods could be interpreted as a secularized expression of Christian love and *diaconia* offered to the neighbor. The Western view on what it means to live a human life in dignity was imbued with Christian ideas and the motivation to reach out and help others and change their life circumstances was also deeply imbued with Christian motivation. This led Christian mission to question NGOs run by Christians

---

17. This tradition cannot be discussed in this short chapter. See *Called to Transformation*, 22–35.

18. Hardiman, "Introduction," 14.

if they show a religious face while pursuing a secular development agenda and secular agencies to ask themselves whether they are a hidden proselytizing project.[19]

In the decades of the second half of the twentieth century the discourses on mission and development have taken different paths. In mission, concepts such as holistic mission,[20] mission as transformation or integral mission which seeks "to act justly, love mercy and walk humbly" (MICAH)[21] have developed. The development discourse, on the other hand, has been increasingly concerned with what has been the activist side of mission, such as supporting and empowering people. The rights-based approach has been widely adopted by Christian development agencies in the Western world.[22] Supporting people's development and empowering them means accompanying them as they seek to claim the rights, they possess but are unable to exercise, including the right to have a religion and to proclaim it to others. The right to freedom of religion or belief "does not include the right to have one's own religion or belief to remain free from criticism or ridicule."[23] The rights-based approach is rooted in human rights and in human dignity—neither of which are Christian concepts but both are deeply informed by the Christian tradition of the human being as the image of God and biblically rooted concepts of justice.[24] This is also evident in the rejection of claims to the universality of human rights with the argument that these concepts are products of the Christian Western world.[25]

We find, on the one hand, a universalist attitude that all people have rights that they deserve to acquire and exercise, including a right to freedom of religion and belief which, in general, is endorsed by mission organizations. However, evangelizing as an invitation to experience a life in Christ and to join the church is in many contexts perceived as asking persons to join a group defined by some particularities which are assumed to separate

---

19. Miles and de Villiers, "Christian NGOs and Their Role in Holistic Mission," 149.
20. Adogame et al., *Engaging the World*.
21. https://micahglobal.org/.
22. Salama and Wiener, "Religion and Human Rights."
23. Quoted from the Rabat Plan of Action (2012) in Salama and Wiener, "Religion and Human Rights," 131.
24. *Called to Transformation*, 42–52.
25. There is an interesting and debated thesis on the impact of mission on the development of democracy in countries in which protestant mission societies have worked: Woodberry, "Missionary Roots of Liberal Democracy."

them from the society at large. How is this perceived tension addressed in mission theology?

An appropriate place to start looking into some of the recent mission discourses in the ecumenical world is *Together Towards Life* (TTL) (2012).[26] TTL states that mission is the love in the Triune God's heart that overflows to all humanity and creation. (§2) "God invites us into the life-giving mission of the Triune God and empowers us to bear witness to the vision of abundant life for all in the new heaven and earth." (§1) Such a life-giving mission is explained to include a concept of life in dignity and TTL therefore proposes as a criterion that "a denial of life is a rejection of the God of life." Faith in the triune God of love and life is particular to the Christians, but the need for life enhancing activities or the promotion of life in dignity is universal. From a Christian perspective, to deprive a human person or a community of such a life is understood as a rejection of the God of life. When people experience this fullness of life, they can experience a glimpse of the God of life.

Witness (*martyria*) to this God "takes concrete form in evangelism—the communication of the whole gospel to the whole of humanity in the whole world. Its goal is the salvation of the world and the glory of the Triune God." (§80) This quotation from the section on evangelism expands upon the earlier definition of mission as promoting life in fullness. It goes on to say that "evangelism is sharing the good news both in word and action." (§83) How can mission then dissolve the assumed tension between the universalist attitude that all people have rights and deserve to exercise them and the supposed particularity that evangelism is an invitation to experience a life in Christ? While verbal proclamation is described as "profoundly biblical," TTL says that evangelism is authentic when the preaching is "consistent with our actions": "The combination of verbal proclamation and visible action bears witness to God's revelation in Jesus Christ and of his purposes." (§83) TTL qualifies further by stating that it is authentic when it is done in a context of dialogue and with an attitude of humility and respect for all. Evangelism and solidarity are like the two sides of a coin—solidarity meaning to join the struggles of the marginalized for their rights.[27] "Christian witness is as much by our presence as by our words. In

---

26. Keum, *Together Towards Life*. Numbers in the text refer to the paragraphs of the document.

27. *Together Towards Life* refers here to "Mission and Evangelism: An Ecumenical Affirmation" from 1982. See "*You Are the Light of the World*," 23.

situations where the public testimony to one's faith is not possible without risking one's life, simply living the gospel may be a powerful alternative" (§89).

We argue that development agencies also have a message which guides their work—empowerment, rights, development, and democracy, and more recently the SDGs. In all of that Christian organizations should be transparent for their Christian foundation and motivation. In 2022 ACT Alliance and the WCC have proposed that ecumenical *diaconia* is the concept which brings together the Christian background and motivation with the development and humanitarian work for all. This is true for churches and for agencies in development. They explain that most organizations of humanitarian aid have, for example, signed a code of conduct that the Red Crescent movement and the Red Cross developed in 1992. The code clarifies that aid is given without furthering a particular religious or political standpoint.[28]

There is a comparable code of conduct for mission which needs to be even more sensitive to the mentioned tension because one dimension of mission is the invitation to join the fellowship of God on earth. *Christian Witness in a Multi-Religious World: Recommendations for Conduct*[29] documents the agreement of the WCC, the Pontifical Council for Interreligious Dialogue, and the World Evangelical Alliance (2011), representing the majority of Christians on the globe, on the understanding of mission, evangelism, and aid. Focusing on witnessing to the "hope that is in us" (1 Pet 3:15), the document speaks about acts of love and service to others "such as providing education, health care, relief services and acts of justice and advocacy are an integral part of witnessing to the gospel" and in so doing "to recognize Christ in the least of their sisters and brothers." We are reminded that in such services, any forms of allurement or of offering incentives are against the gospel.[30] The main argument is that the "vulnerability of people and their need for healing" should not be exploited. On the other hand, human rights and the freedom for religion and belief are endorsed.[31]

---

28. *Called to Transformation*, 113–14.
29. *Christian Witness in a Multi-Religious World*.
30. *Christian Witness in a Multi-Religious World*, principle 4.
31. *Christian Witness in a Multi-Religious World*, principle 7.

DEVELOPMENT AND EVANGELISM

Although many churches engage in projects and activities that today are framed in a rights-based framework and promote development, it seems that the professionalization and the establishment of both Christian and secular development agencies has led to a universalization of development and a particularization of mission as if mission is only evangelism. As shown, mission has the focus on "life in its fullness" for all already in this world—but is accused of instrumentalizing its diaconical or development efforts to make converts.

Even though churches as faith-based organizations have come to be seen as partners in development, they have to be careful that their development work for all is not confused with the invitation for all to come to Christ. The secular development discourse can reinforce the perception of mission history as a movement pressuring people to convert and manipulating their consciousness. As a result, mission seems to be reduced in the past and the present to motivating people to change their religious identity and affiliation. TTL as a reflection on mission shows that there is more to mission and we will conclude with three learning experiences of the ecumenical mission movement.

The modern movement in which Protestant churches and missionary societies have been so deeply involved began with a sense of superiority. Over the course of more than two hundred years and with the foundation of churches in the non-Western world and particularly in the ecumenical fellowship with much older churches in these regions, the movement has learned that the focus is on the contextual realities of the local communities, not on the missionary. This means that what constitutes a life in fullness or in dignity can vary from context to context and needs to be developed by the local communities in the fellowship of a truly "catholic" church. This includes taking into account and respecting the spiritual dimensions of transformation which should accompany the improvement of living conditions. The debates on gospel and culture, inculturation and contextualization offer a wealth of insights and experiences from which development agencies can also benefit.

The widely shared belief that God was there before the missionary (perceived as a foreigner to the culture) (TTL, §94) offers a perspective for doing both development and evangelism when both are rooted in local realities. Local traditions and beliefs can be appreciated and values and concepts of community life can be the basis for contextualizing the rights and responsibilities of people as they work to improve their living conditions.

However, mission theology offers an important aspect deeply rooted in the belief in the triune God of life. Human attempts to create a better life through development do not always and everywhere succeed. Mission is not only about experiencing life in dignity and progress, it is also about building resistance and resilience in catastrophic situations and coping with suffering, failure, and the feeling of being left behind. This is a dimension in which the foundation of mission in God transcends all human efforts and sanctifies the individual and life that seems to fail according to human standards. Being rooted in a deeper reality, Christian faith can free Christian development work from being condemned to succeed by human standards.

In the light of these learning experiences, TTL and *Christian Witness in a Multi-Religious World* offer a criterion for discerning how the services offered might be provided. Therefore, mission properly understood is well aware of a solution to the tension discussed here. Mission as evangelism with the aim of inviting people to a life with Christ and to join a church are at risk to be identified with seducing or luring people into their fold, in the worst case through pressure. It is obvious, however, that this cannot be a Christian attitude, for someone who nominally professes Christ cannot be considered to be a Christian. If someone professes faith this must be serious and based on an inner certainty. This perspective is deeply rooted in the Reformed theology that faith and the transformation into a "new creature" is a gift of the Spirit and not the result of one's own actions. This strengthens the ability to distinguish between the experience of charity or empowerment in one's own community and joining a new community for the pure reason to receive goods.

Mission is doing itself harm if it focuses only on evangelism because it then risks being accused of focusing only on the future salvation of the soul while neglecting the body in life before death. On the other hand, if the services are secularized to the extent of not transpiring the light in which the current state of the affairs is analyzed and evaluated nor the motivation of those who engage in it, they lose their Christian soul. Holistic or integrated mission can engage with issues such as the climate crisis. Firstly, because Christians too are affected by it, secondly, because congregations are to be found all over the world, in dramatically afflicted regions and also in less afflicted regions. Thirdly, the global fellowship of these congregations hinges on solidarity and mutual support. Fourthly, from the history of services offered by mission it is evident that this solidarity was never meant exclusively for Christians alone. In our entangled world, we think that mission needs to have a second look at approaches in what is called "reverse mission" to address issues of underdevelopment and injustices of marginalized migrant communities (see ch. 6) in the host countries.[32] We understand mission to encompass a cooperation with all people of good will for the promotion of the common good, emphasizing the dignity of everyone and their right for life in abundance, promised to all creation and every creature.

---

32. Drønen, "Christian Mission and International Development," 269, also proposes to do so.

5

The People We Need to Become

Risto: Kenneth, we are living in a time when many people express their identity without any need to belong to a religion. Churches in the Global North are decreasing. You are currently based in the Global South where churches are growing. What makes you continue to identify as a Christian?

Kenneth: I too have known times when I doubted if faith makes sense. But I come back to the words of Peter to Jesus: "Lord, to whom else would we go? You have the words of eternal life." There is so much in Christianity that I find to be life giving and inspiring.

Risto: Faith is admittedly a strong support for life, but there are many other dimensions and themes that people find inspiring and motivating and supporting in life. Does your faith really make any difference when it comes to the everyday life?

Kenneth: I am quite political in outlook, and I have been highly motivated at times by political movements. In the end, though, they always disappoint. I find that my faith connects me to something that never disappoints—the presence and the promises of God.

Risto: If something never disappoints, it surely is attractive and unique in the world that we live in. How would you say your faith been sustained and nourished by Christians in the Global South?

Kenneth: I have been fortunate to live for many years in Malawi where I have met many people whose faith is stronger than my own. The way they draw on their faith to meet the adversities of life has made a big impact on me.

When I am weak in my faith, I am carried along by the solidarity of big-hearted Malawian Christians.

Risto: This sounds fabulous! There is so much we can learn from other Christians, and vice versa. Being together we make one another stronger. In addition to the growing world Christianity, in particular in Africa, are there any new developments that have encouraged you in your faith?

Kenneth: Yes, one thing that has had a big impact on me is the fresh thinking about the meaning of Christian faith that has been generated recently in the ecumenical movement. Especially a call to transforming discipleship that was issued by a World Mission Conference at Arusha in 2018—it has demonstrated the relevance of a faith perspective in meeting the challenges of life today.

Risto: Churches in the Global South and ecumenical mission movement are strong actors that have had great impact on your life. But not all Christians have a contact with them. In general, do you think that faith can still make a difference in our contemporary world?

Kenneth: I think it can. But as people of faith, we need to be transformed ourselves before we can hope to make a meaningful difference in our world.

NOTWITHSTANDING THE POWER AND influence of conservative and reactionary forces, there is a broad consensus today that there is need for radical change in the relationship between people and planet, in the way we organize ourselves economically and politically, and in our understanding of ourselves and our neighbors. As Rebecca Tarbotton of the Rainforest Action Network has observed: "We need to remember that the work of our time is bigger than climate change. We need to be setting our sights higher and deeper. What we're really talking about, if we're honest with ourselves, is transforming everything about the way we live on this planet."[1] If such transformation is to occur, if our reality is to become something very different from what it is today, we need to begin with ourselves. For, before it is anything else, our crisis is a crisis of the human person.

We talk about climate crisis (see ch. 2) but what is behind the climate crisis? Of course, it is human action. It is human behavior that has caused the crisis, and it is because of human folly that we fail to address it. Grappling with the reality of catastrophic climate change led Naomi Klein to the conclusion that, "The solution to global warming is not to fix the world, it is

---

1. Cited in Klein, *This Changes Everything*, v.

to fix ourselves."[2] The same applies to the global economic crisis—what has caused it if not human greed and avarice? It might seem like an impossible dream to imagine there could be a different kind of human person. But this is the vision that lies at the heart of the Christian faith. As the apostle Paul put it, "If anyone is in Christ, they are a new creation; old things are passed away; behold all things are become new" (2 Cor 5:17). Might this biblical vision turn out to be a crucial contribution to inspiring the imagination we need today? It invites us to explore the possibility of our humanity being renewed and transformed in a way that equips us to meet the extraordinary challenges of this moment in history.

The Fourth Industrial Revolution is now upon us, with technological innovation advancing rapidly and the development of artificial intelligence, in the words of Klaus Schwab, "not only changing the 'what' and the 'how' of doing things, but also 'who' we are."[3] This poses profound questions for the future of human identity and vocation. Seong-Won Park spells out what is at stake: "The era when human beings controlled machines is going by, and the era of machines controlling humans is arriving. What might our life look like in this era? What will it mean to be human beings and what will be the place of human spirituality?"[4] The power imbalances already apparent in the human community could take a sinister turn if the use of artificial intelligence empowers some while victimizing others.[5] Given humanity's propensity for injustice and oppression, excitement about the positive possibilities of artificial intelligence (AI) is tempered by concern about how it could be deployed in damaging and destructive ways. What will be the place of Christian and other religious traditions in a world that increasingly revolves around artificial intelligence?

When it comes to the decisive question of how we understand our humanity, the religious vision has often been contrasted with a more secular construction. The former tends to be cast as backward, primitive, and divisive while the latter is seen as progressive, enlightened, and unifying. A widely prevalent intellectual analysis regards religion as prejudiced, irrational, and bigoted while a secular approach to life is seen as objective, rational, and tolerant. On closer inspection, however, it appears today that abandonment of a religious vision of life tends to lead to the embrace of

---

2. Klein, *This Changes Everything*, 279.
3. Cited in Park, *Humanity and Spirituality*, 12.
4. Park, *Humanity and Spirituality*.
5. See Mshana, "Human Mind and Heart and Artificial Intelligence."

another faith system, one which has succeeded in establishing itself as the belief structure around which the global economy is organized. This is often described as neoliberalism—a belief that market forces not only hold the solution to the quest for prosperity but also answer the question of the nature of human identity. It is a system that puts a premium on material prosperity and individuality with the result that the profit motive becomes the driving force of human life and the means of human fulfillment. As Jung Mo Sung argues, "Secularization did not mean the end of the gods and religions, but rather the replacement of God's sovereignty as the foundation of society and of eschatological promises by the notion of popular sovereignty, and later, by the notion of economic rationality of the market as the foundation of society and the promises of the myth of progress."[6]

What meets us today in the swirl of contemporary life is not so much a contest between a religious and non-religious understanding of the world. It is more like a choice between two belief systems. For neoliberalism is guided by a vision of what is ultimately true about human life, has formed certain core convictions in this regard, and maintains these even when the evidence does not support them. The economic system built on the basis of the neoliberal vision meets two great challenges today. The evidence is that it promotes an exploitative approach to the natural world that is unsustainable and that it has an exclusionary effect in the human community so that, while it brings great rewards to the few, it results in deprivation and desperation for the many. Far from leading to widespread human flourishing, it appears to have unleashed destructive forces that threaten not only our human future but even the earth itself. Is it not high time to have a conversation about the structure of belief that underpins the neoliberal system? Is it correct that humanity is defined by individualism, selfishness, and greed? Is it true that self-gratification is the essential motivation for the living of human life?

The Christian vision is one that firmly challenges such assumptions. Martin Luther King Jr. offered a prophetic word to our times when he declared: "We must rapidly begin the shift from a 'thing-oriented society' to a 'person-oriented society.' When machines and computers, profit motives and property rights, are considered more important than people, the giant triplets of racism, extreme materialism, and militarism are incapable of

---

6. Sung, *Desire, Market and Religion*, 56.

being conquered."[7] The subsequent years have witnessed a remorseless advance of the "three giant triplets," causing untold suffering and devastation.

The core narrative of Christianity begins with an affirmation of our common humanity, recognizing that every human person has inalienable, God-given dignity. It acknowledges that something has gone wrong with our human life but insists that this is not the end of the story. God has acted, particularly through the coming of Jesus Christ at the heart of our history, to set right what had gone wrong. Jesus came with a promise to heal, renew, and restore our human life. The Spirit of God is active in our world today to bring about the fulfillment of this promise. Hence there is always hope. Though there are times when we could be tempted to despair of the prospects for humanity when we are exposed to the human capacity for hatred, greed, and violence, the perspective of Christian faith is a hopeful one. No matter how much any human situation might be prey to the forces of death, Christ promises life.

This vision of human life and destiny might be a potentially transformative one but there are formidable obstacles that prevent it from taking effect. Christianity as an organized religion has often failed to be true to its founding vision. In fact, it has been complicit in many of the destructive forces that are most threatening today. It has found expression in ways that are exploitative and exclusionary, echoing the neoliberal system more than challenging it. In European countries with a long Christian tradition, there are many who no longer find the faith convincing. Even those who identify as Christians are aware that the way the faith has been framed in earlier generations does not connect well with the way we live and think today. There is therefore a need to rethink the faith in relation to our contemporary crisis, which is what this book is seeking to do. One step we can take is to engage with the inward dimension of human life and identity, sometimes described as spirituality.

ON A SPIRITUAL WAVELENGTH

As the ecumenical movement has wrestled with how to understand its missionary mandate in this new century, it has placed a premium on thinking in terms of the action of the Spirit of God. This was already apparent at the Athens World Mission Conference of the World Council of Churches

---

7. Cited in Klein, *This Changes Everything*, 449.

(WCC), held in 2005,[8] and came to fuller expression in the major WCC mission affirmation *Together Towards Life* (TTL), published in 2012. Rather than thinking of mission in terms of institutions or strategies, it proposes, "Life in the Holy Spirit is the essence of mission, the core of why we do what we do and how we live our lives. Spirituality gives the deepest meaning to our lives and motivates our actions. It is a sacred gift from the Creator, the energy for affirming and caring for life."[9] In this perspective, mission is not so much a project as a way of being, a way of living. In a world crying out for authenticity, people of faith are challenged to demonstrate their identity and vocation in the way they live. This in turn creates an openness among people of all faiths and none, shared humanity bringing us together and breaking down barriers.

Such an expansive vision will surely be needed if the challenges facing our world today are to be met. After decades of examining the question of how Christian faith might be a force for reconciliation in situations of conflict, Robert Schreiter concluded that it is more a matter of spirituality than of strategy.[10] It is a point that has wider application. Strategy has its place, but it also has its limits. In many situations it is a whole new way of being human that is needed. It is authentic spirituality that can make the difference. Pope Paul VI detected something important about our time when he wrote that "men and women listen more willingly to witnesses than to teachers, and if they listen to teachers, it is because they are witnesses."[11]

In today's context, as people search for identity and meaning, institutional authority counts for little. It is when people speak out of their own lived experience that their message cuts through. Korean theologian Kyo-Seong Ahn has proposed that, in contrast to the "orthodoxy" or "orthopraxis" that defined religion in earlier times, today what is required is "orthopathy." This involves proclaiming the message "not from the head, not from the hand, but from the heart." Its keynotes are relationship, emotional intelligence, symbiosis, interdependence, pathos, and respect.[12] There is no room here for aggression or self-aggrandizement. Humility and mutuality become the qualities that count. These are needed not only to redefine our relationships with one another but also with the environment around us.

8. Matthey, "*Come Holy Spirit, Heal and Reconcile!*"
9. Keum, *Together Towards Life*, §3.
10. Schreiter, *Ministry of Reconciliation*.
11. Cited in Bevans and Schroeder, *Constants in Context*, 352.
12. Ahn, "From Mission to Church and Beyond," 74–84.

As Pope Francis urges, "Let us stop thinking, then, of human beings as autonomous, omnipotent and limitless, and begin to think of ourselves differently, in a humbler but more fruitful way."[13] The future might depend on how far we are able to undergo such a transformation. Who in the context of today's world is not aware of the need for a different way of thinking and acting? Whether our analysis is political, economic, ecological, or personal it is likely to tell us that what is needed is not some gentle amelioration but rather something that can be a game changer.

TRANSFORMING DISCIPLES

As churches across the world have attempted to imagine such transformation during the early years of the twenty-first century, they have turned to what might be an unexpected source. They have discovered fresh resonance in the biblical idea of discipleship. Those who heard the call of Jesus, took the decision to follow him, and brought their lives under his influence and inspiration, were described as disciples. They themselves underwent a process of transformation—for example, impetuous Peter became a rock-like character. As a result, they became agents of transformation, known as people "who had turned the world upside down" (Acts 17:6). As the global context calls for a recovery of authentic spirituality, not to escape from harsh realities but to confront and transform them, the idea of discipleship has struck a chord.

Among the first to give expression to this was Pope Benedict XVI when he suggested to the Aparecida Conference of the Latin American Catholic Bishops in 2007 that Christians, "by virtue of their Baptism . . . are called to be disciples and missionaries of Jesus Christ. This implies following him, living in intimacy with him, imitating his example and bearing witness."[14] A prominent figure at Aparecida was Cardinal Jorge Bergoglio who later succeeded Benedict when he became Pope Francis in 2013. He set the tone for his pontificate with his apostolic exhortation *Evangelii Gaudium*, which echoed the language and emphases of the Aparecida Conference. In particular, it brought together the question of mission and that of discipleship: "Every Christian is a missionary to the extent that he or she has encountered

---

13. Pope Francis, *Laudate Deum*, §68.
14. Cited in Bevans, *Community of Missionary Disciples*, 317.

the love of God in Christ Jesus: we no longer say that we are 'disciples' and 'missionaries,' but rather that we are always 'missionary disciples.'"[15]

This language, at first sight, might seem unconvincing. Missionaries have had a bad press, often portrayed as arrogant cultural imperialists. Disciple is an almost forgotten term, its connotation of discipline sounding discordant at a time when personal freedom is highly prized. Yet it is with the retrieval of these terms and their application to the challenges of our day that Pope Francis identified his point of engagement. Soon it became apparent that this line of thinking resonated with Christians in many different ecclesial traditions. The crisis of authenticity experienced in the twenty-first century could be addressed by bringing together two seminal strands of the Christian faith: the missionary mandate and the call to become disciples. Without the Christ-like way of life that is discovered on the path of discipleship any missionary endeavor is going to lack credibility. When a thousand Christian leaders gathered in Arusha, Tanzania, in 2018 for a World Mission Conference under the auspices of the WCC, they "had to reckon with death-dealing forces that are shaking the world order and inflicting suffering on many."[16] As they reflected on how they might be a force for change they brought the idea of discipleship to center stage, proposing that this might be the driver of the transformation that our world so desperately needs.

Among the advantages of thinking in terms of discipleship is that this concept held the promise that it could overcome a longstanding polarization within Christianity, particularly in its Protestant expression. During the twentieth century a wide gulf opened up between those who thought of the faith in terms of personal conversion and those who thought more in terms of the transformation of society. Thinking through the meaning of discipleship has led to a recognition that it is a matter of both/and, not either/or.[17] In fact, the life of discipleship involves a deepening of both dimensions. As Luis Wesley de Souza has put it: "There must be no mission without spiritual contemplation and experimentation of Christ's life in us, and there is no authentic Christian spirituality that does not translate itself into prophetic imagination, mission cooperation, and engagement."[18]

---

15. Pope Francis, *Evangelii Gaudium*, §120.
16. Jukko and Keum, *Moving in the Spirit*, 2.
17. See Ross, "Arusha Call," 443–57.
18. de Souza, "Spirituality," 264.

The People We Need to Become

First and foremost, to be a disciple of Jesus Christ is a matter of inward transformation. This goes far beyond institutional affiliation or formal identity. It is about embarking on a spiritual journey. It is about an inward encounter with Christ, the formation of Christ-like character and embarking on a way of life that corresponds with the path that Jesus followed. In the words of the WCC's "Arusha Call to Discipleship," it is a "Christ-connected way of life."[19] Pope Francis captures what this means in terms of the immediate experience of faith: "I invite all Christians, everywhere, at this very moment, to a renewed personal encounter with Jesus Christ, or at least an openness to letting him encounter them; I ask all of you to do this unfailingly each day."[20] Any outward engagement must spring from this inward commitment, cultivated by such spiritual practices as personal prayer and communal worship. These in turn shape character, form attitudes, and guide action. Here is the indispensable inner spring of the transformation promised by Christ.

As this inward transformation takes place, disciples are, at the same time, shaped so as to become agents of transformation. The inward spiritual transformation necessarily leads to the outward engagement that is conventionally described as "mission." As ecumenical mission leader Lesslie Newbigin expressed it: "There is no participation in Christ without participation in his mission to the world."[21] Today, many would agree that our world is in need of mission in the sense that the human community's mode of operation needs to become very different from the way things are now. Therefore, there is a need for agents of change—"missionaries." This is not any narrowly conceived mission for it is as wide as the presence of God and as broad as the purposes of God. A missionary orientation is, by its very nature, a matter of transformation. It is not content to settle for the status quo but, whatever the situation, it is oriented to its transformation in the direction of the kingdom of God.

This book takes its bearings from Jesus Christ and the transformation that he promised. But it is also inspired by openness to the adventure of discerning the action of the Spirit of God who constantly takes us by surprise. Far from promoting an exclusive, intolerant, or bigoted approach to others, this missionary orientation forms people who are open, curious, and eager to make common cause in resisting the forces that make for death

---

19. "Arusha Call to Discipleship," 2.
20. Pope Francis, *Evangelii Gaudium*, §3.
21. Newbigin, *Open Secret*, 1.

and embracing those that make for life. Rather than thinking of mission as a competitive or aggressive enterprise that aims to "defeat" people of other faiths, the mission impetus needed today is one that empowers the human community to pull together in meeting grave threats to its very existence. As the WCC World Mission Conference at Arusha discovered, "Discipleship is an invitation both to a relationship and to a vocation. A relationship that is humble, vulnerable and mutual, and finds itself growing in following Christ, in Christ's own ways, and in finding God at work in situations of strife and struggle, and in empowering people to resist and transform structures and cultures in the name of the Triune God. It is, therefore, a vocation of collaborating with God for the transformation of the world."[22]

TIME TO MOVE TOGETHER

The neoliberal global economy runs on an exclusive basis, privileging the few and excluding the many. Authentic Christian witness is to exactly the opposite—to the kingdom of Christ where all are welcome, especially the least and the lost. Not only in our words but in our actions, we need to cultivate togetherness. We need to be *together* in transformation. One thing that the ecumenical mission movement has demonstrated again and again is that it is the relational quality of human life that enables us to flourish. The deeper we go in our relations with one another, especially with those with whom we have had differences, the greater our discovery of what our human personhood means.

It must be acknowledged, however, that the missionary work of the churches has often been portrayed as doing the very opposite of cultivating togetherness. It has been seen as arrogant, aggressive, and divisive. It has been criticized, often justifiably, for disparaging and denigrating the traditions of others in order to impose its own understanding. Contemporary understanding of mission, however, has fostered a very different approach. Stephen Bevans observes that there has been "a fundamental shift from a missiology of power to a missiology of relationship and vulnerability."[23] Instead of conceiving of mission as a human activity where we aim to advance the interests of our group, it has recognized that, in its deepest sense, mission is about the action of God. It is about the reign of God (kingdom of God) of which Jesus spoke. It is about the wide horizons of the activity

---

22. "Arusha Conference Report," 9.
23. Bevans, "From Edinburgh to Edinburgh," 8.

of the Holy Spirit who "works in the world often in mysterious and unknown ways beyond our imagination."[24] Mission then is not something that is under our control or about asserting our agenda. Instead, it involves the humble posture of recognizing that we have become involved in something much bigger than ourselves. The wonder of grace is that God calls women and men to play a part in the unfolding of the divine purposes, but they need to be modest about their own role and open to what they can learn from others.

As Bevans observes from a Catholic perspective, "Mission needs to be understood not so much as a mission ad *gentes*—implying that missionaries or ministers bring something ready-made and new to peoples in the world. Rather, today mission must be envisioned as mission inter *gentes*—living among peoples, respecting their histories and cultures, appreciating their religions and customs, open to every other disciple in the community, ready to be enriched and challenged by them."[25] Relationship and mutuality here become the keynotes: mission *with* more than mission *to*. This creates an openness to connect with others and a readiness to make common cause. As Bevans and Schroeder suggest, "In a world where the Spirit is constantly manifest in social and political movements, in the riches of culture, and in the holiness of many religious ways, mission can serve that Spirit only through acts of justice, trust of human experience, and dialogue with religious difference."[26] Evangelism then becomes a two-way process of mutual enrichment, common ground is found, shared action can be initiated and the reign of God can come in ways least expected.

The importance of the relational dimension has been highlighted in the life of the Catholic Church by its recent emphasis on "synodality," which has been described as the "leitmotif" of Pope Francis's pontificate.[27] In essence, this is about the church becoming less "top-down" and more "bottom-up." As Bevans explains: "Synodality is lived out in the conviction that the church is first of all a *communion*—a community of disciples who are fundamentally equal because of baptism. It is with that conviction that all in the church are called to *participation*, honestly yet humbly expressing their experiences of faith and opinions of how the church should be and act in the world. Then, through a process of deep listening and discernment,

---

24. Keum, *Together Towards Life*, §15.
25. Bevans, "'Your Light Must Shine Before Others,'" 173.
26. Bevans and Schroeder, *Prophetic Dialogue*, 81.
27. Gaillardetz, "Implementing Synodality," 100.

the church community moves to decisions about *mission*."[28] The primary expression of synodality is within the church as members relate to one another and build their agency together. At the same time, this cultivates an attitude of openness that extends far beyond the confines of the church. "No one is excluded; all are welcome and encouraged to participate—women, men, youth, homeless, poor, prisoners, disaffected, and where appropriate, other Christians, members of other faiths, those of no faith."[29]

To be a disciple of Christ is to be drawn into community. It is to step into a way of life where relationship building and dialogue are essential, where differences are seen as enriching, and where boundary-crossing skills are cultivated and promoted. Such a way of life finds expression today also on digital platforms as people everywhere are drawn into virtual connections and networks. As artificial intelligence develops, we begin to see the emergence of a metaverse where interactions occur on an entirely virtual basis.[30] This will undoubtedly bring new challenges in terms of understanding the nature of our humanity and fulfilling our human vocation. Korean theologian Seong-Won Park has insisted that a relational epistemology will be crucial to meeting the challenges of AI.[31] The words of the WCC Arusha Conference might prove to be prophetic: "In a world that prizes individuality, at a time when society is increasingly atomized, and in a context where people are polarized by identity politics, Christ calls his disciples to community. Following him means moving away from a self-centered life to find fulfillment in generous self-giving—the way of Christ. The journey is one that transforms and shapes the lives of others; a journey not to be made alone, but together. Discipleship is not only vertical but also horizontal in its scope and expression."[32] The transformation entailed in discipleship is one that opens us up to others in ways we might never have imagined.

---

28. Bevans, "'Your Light Must Shine Before Others,'" 171.
29. Bevans, "'Your Light Must Shine Before Others,'" 172.
30. See Jun, "Mission in the Age of Digitalization," 241–60.
31. Park, *Humanity and Spirituality*, 20.
32. "Arusha Conference Report," 14.

6

The Migration We Need to Welcome

Kenneth: Marina, are you a migrant?

Marina: Yes, moving from one place to another for work I certainly count among the migrants. Coming from the Northeast of India, I have lived and worked in South India, Geneva/Bossey and am currently living in the UK.

Kenneth: What are the questions which come with that status?

Marina: Obviously, one important question is the language and luckily for me English has become a global language. Without knowledge of the local language, you remain an outsider, even within the same country—like India. A question important to me is what does home mean. I realize that I still consider Mizoram not only as my place of origin but as my home, even though I have lived longer outside the state than in Mizoram.

Kenneth: What about the legal issues?

Marina: The countries where I have lived have strict regulations for migrants and most are connected to the issue of work. As long as you have work, you can have a legal status. Whenever I travel by plane, I have to check in at the counter for visa verification. My Indian passport is ranked eighty-fifth in the Henley Global Passport Index.[1] It gives me visa-free access to fifty-seven countries in Asia, Oceania, Africa, and the Caribbean. However, most of them are not countries to which I usually am invited for conferences. Applying for citizenship in the UK, my new passport would rank third and would allow me to visit 189 countries without a visa, this time

---

1. Henley Passport Index.

including apparently all European countries and many more. With a UK passport, I would be privileged compared to a passport holder from South Africa (place 83 on the list) or Nigeria (95) or Afghanistan (107), with Iraq, Syria, and Pakistan at the bottom of the list (104–107), interestingly below North Korea.

Ken: *What about other aspects of being a migrant?*

Marina: *In the European Union and the UK, I observe a polarization on the issue of migrants. The countries need migrants for their work force and for demographic reasons but in their societies the voices rejecting any person from outside for whatever reason as an unwelcome outsider are getting louder.*

Kenneth: *What is the relation of migration to mission?*

Marina: *In the last decades, theology rediscovered migration as a characteristic of the Christian history, so much that some speak of migration being in the DNA of the Christian faith. This does not yet help to overcome the separation in the Christian fold into local and migrant churches. I see here a challenge for mission, both for the local churches and those churches or fellowships of migrants.*

"BIRTH LOTTERY" AND THE WEB OF MOVEMENT

THE WORLD MIGRATION REPORT (2022) states: "Examining the overall quality of life by country, and the ability to migrate in terms of visa access, reveals that the availability of migration options is partly related to the lottery of birth and in particular the national passport of the potential migrant. For instance, some nationality groups appear to be much less likely to have access to visas and visa-free arrangements."[2]

According to the Report, 281 million people do not live in their country of origin. Most of them come both from countries with weaker passports—if they have any at all—and are trying to enter countries to which their passport does not easily allow them to travel. Traveling and migration legalized by agreements between states is at odds with the larger movements of people on the globe. Two hundred eighty-one million is a large number but it represents only 3.6 percent of the world's population; a much larger number are internal migrants. More than 40 percent of transnational

---

2. International Organization for Migration, *World Migration Report*, 194.

migrants come from Asian countries, with the largest group being of Indian origin. Many migrate to the USA or the UK, but also in large numbers to Saudi Arabia and other Gulf states. In 2020, Indian families received $83.15 billion in remittances from family members who had migrated to other countries.[3] Many South Indians work in the Emirates and the phenomenon of Filipino women who work in households all over Asia is well known.

Another face of migration is the refugee. Large numbers of people are fleeing catastrophic situations such as war, displacement, persecution, or climate crisis–induced effects like famine and drought. According to the UN Refugee Agency, 117.3 million people were forcibly displaced by mid-2024.[4] Of those 68.3 million are internally displaced[5] and 43.4 million are refugees crossing borders.[6]

Most refugees in Asia end up in neighboring countries, such as Afghans in Pakistan, or Rohingya from Myanmar in Bangladesh.[7] The largest refugee camp of the world is said to be found in Bangladesh (952,000, as of the end of 2022), close to the Myanmar border (mainly Rohingya); other large camps are in some regions in Africa.[8] The Northeast Indian State of Mizoram is currently hosting refugees from the neighboring Myanmar and from the state of Manipur where violent and deadly clashes began in May 2023.

An important dimension of migration is the increasing impact of climate change. The World Migration Report devotes an entire chapter to the complexities of livelihood degradation and the movement of people, both within countries and across national borders.[9] This chapter also provides recommendations for addressing climate-induced migration within the implementation of the United Nations Framework Convention on Climate Change (UNFCCC).[10] It mentions some regional agreements on relocation, such as those in the Pacific, some African states, and Latin America.[11]

---

3. International Organization for Migration, *World Migration Report*, 41.
4. UNHCR, "About UNHCR."
5. UNHCR, "Who We Protect: Internally Displaced People."
6. UNHCR, "Who We Protect: Refugees."
7. UNHCR, "About UNHCR."
8. Numbers and information are taken from the different reports found at UNHCR, "About UNHCR."
9. International Organization for Migration, *World Migration Report*, 233–52.
10. International Organization for Migration, *World Migration Report*, 241.
11. International Organization for Migration, *World Migration Report*, 248–50.

However, it points out that many people who leave their homes and cross national borders due to climate-related changes are currently counted as economic migrants, failing to recognize the true reason for their movement.[12] Identifying the climate crisis as a reason for migration and linking its global impact with respective legislation within national frameworks is one of the future tasks of migration debates.

To reflect on mission and migration in this context, we need to take different aspects into account. Both flight and migration have existed throughout history. Today, in a globalized era goods and capital flow much more freely across the globe than people can move. Since the beginning of the twenty-first century global flows have changed considerably with the movements of migrants. States have made stronger attempts to restrict the entry of migrants, as well as increased attempts at "securitization."[13] The second aspect is that "research on migration in the Global South is a rather new field and in-depth studies analysing religion and migration are few. To date, most theories about religion and migration have been developed in relation to Europe and North America."[14]

As it can be seen, there is more to do here. In this chapter, we will focus on migrants who cross international borders for a variety of reasons, and how they practice their faith.

MISSION FROM THE MARGINS

For refugees and migrants, the role played by religion in their experience may vary. Refugees may be fleeing for religious reasons,[15] and some may find in religion a resource that strengthens their resilience. They may also find material support in the transnational networks of their religious community. Focusing on those who migrate, whether legally or illegally, brings other aspects into the picture. Nowadays, migration has diversified, meaning that people move to other countries and stay or return after a while or move on to another country. One effect is that particularly in countries

---

12. International Organization for Migration, *World Migration Report*, 240.
13. Nordin and Otterbeck, *Migration and Religion*, 4.
14. Nordin and Otterbeck, *Migration and Religion*, 4.
15. "Reasons for migration also most certainly affect religion; fleeing because of one's religiosity or moving between two countries with similar religious contexts and being vaguely religious, probably affect people's religiosity in different ways." Nordin and Otterbeck, *Migration and Religion*, 9.

where the extended family is quite common, members of such family networks may live and work in different countries. In this way, migration creates transnational networks in which migrants stay in touch with people at home, even more so in the age of the internet and social media. Through online connections they are more likely to find people like themselves in the destination country.

Migrants bring their religion with them and in many cases practice it. An interesting question is the extent to which religion may begin to play a more important role in the lives of migrants in their new country compared to their home country, as a way of living out one's cultural identity in a different context. An important question for migrants is how their assumed culture and religion is viewed in the host countries. Their faith can be a resource for coping with the challenges of living abroad, including the mutual support they may find in the religious communities. For example, it is a different question for Hindus from India to practice their religion in the UK, now home to the two largest Hindu temples outside India,[16] than it is for Indian Mizo living in the UK who are Christians.

Some among the migrants spread their religion in a variety of ways, for instance by practicing it visibly such as in the cited case of Hindus in the UK, or by actively propagating it, as some Muslim organizations do. The UK Islamic Mission names as its main objective to respond to "the immediate religious needs of the new migrant Muslim community in the UK" but is also "producing basic literature on Islam in English." Additionally, it raises funds for emergency help, mainly in dominantly Islamic countries.[17]

In the case of migrants related to the Christian faith, the country of residence may offer them the opportunity to practice their faith freely, as in the case of oppressed communities, or to adopt a new faith, which they were unable to do in their country of origin. There are significant numbers of people from Afghanistan, Iran, or the Gulf States who have adopted Christianity while residing in another country.

Against this diverse background, what can be said of migration from a Christian perspective and of Christian migrants as missionaries? *Together Towards Life* (TTL) introduces the topic by relating it to the shift in Christianity's center of gravity, reminding us that Christian mission had been conceptualized as a movement of expansion from centers to "unreached territories." In the current period of world Christianity in

---

16. https://londonmandir.baps.org/ and https://www.venkateswara.org.uk/.
17. See the APPEALS on https://www.ukim.org/.

which the majority of Christians live in the Global South "migration has become a worldwide, multi-directional phenomenon which is reshaping the Christian landscape." How does this shift of gravity impact mission and evangelism and how does it affect missionary practices and theologies (§5)?

TTL transforms the traditional spatial movement of mission(aries) into a reversal of the direction of movement between socially defined groups: from the marginalized to the privileged. It recalls that God had chosen the poor and powerless (1 Cor 1:18–31) "to further God's mission of justice and peace so that life may flourish. If there is a shift of the mission concept from 'mission *to* the margins' to 'mission *from* the margins,' what then is the distinctive contribution of the people from the margins?" (§6) Although the margin was introduced as a spatial concept, TTL transforms it into a socially and epistemologically defined term. Against a notion of mission as the movement from the privileged to the marginalized, TTL highlights that people at the margins have agency. They own what has been called an epistemological privilege, to perceive from their position at the margins which forces effect their exclusion and produce the privileges others enjoy. Their mission is to uncover these hidden structures and to address them so that life may flourish (§38).

A surprising observation is, that while "margin" and its derivatives appear more than seventy times in the document, migration is mentioned only four times in the document (§5, §70, §76). Migrants as persons appear only once in the whole document—and migrants and their community are spoken of as those who are vulnerable and in need of support and to whom the local congregations should offer hospitality. TTL suggests that by integrating migrants, local congregations could create a "multi-cultural ministry and mission as a concrete expression of common witness in diversity." (§70) In the section on the local congregation, we read that migrants could help the local churches to "re-discover themselves afresh." Together, they could find "exciting opportunities for contextual expressions of intercultural mission" (§75).

TTL argues here from the position of the local churches. By integrating migrants, the church could become a local expression of the multicultural character of the global Christian community. Its mission is to become "a concrete expression of common witness in diversity" in its context. Christian migrants or migrants becoming Christians are thus seen as a source of renewal for the local community. We should not expect to find all the answers in TTL to possible questions, such as how these multicultural congregations relate to the denominational and confessional fabric and logics in their localities. However, what seems to be missing in TTL's approach is the question of what transforming influence migrants might have on the local congregations. Insofar as they are vulnerable as migrants or have the epistemological privilege of perceiving what forces of exclusion are at work, they can enlighten the local congregations about the social and political fabric of their societies. TTL recognizes the emergence of strong Pentecostal and charismatic movements as a most remarkable feature of today's world Christianity. One wonders whether the Pentecostalization and charismatization of local congregations would be one effect of such an influx of Christian migrants?

BRINGING BACK THE GOSPEL

None of what has been said so far corresponds to or addresses the concept of reverse mission. Three of the top ten countries sending the largest numbers of missionaries are today in the Global South—Brazil, South Korea, and India. The number of the destination countries is limited and does not always seem to be chosen according to the highest proportion of non-Christians in the population.[18]

There is considerable literature on reverse mission in Europe with an African background.[19] A recent study addresses South Korean missionaries sent to the UK, and in doing so, touches upon several aspects that have been discussed previously. The South Korean missiologist Sinwoong Kim, now based in Birmingham, UK, writes that between 1979 and 2017 the number of mission agencies—parachurch and denominational—in South Korea increased from 21 to 227. In addition to missionaries those ministries have sent, a large number of independent missionaries, for example supported by individual congregations in South Korea, came to the UK (24–25).[20]

Kim explores the beliefs of Korean missionaries who see themselves as bringing back the gospel to evangelize the English. They work among what Kim calls "people on the edge of the church," ordinary people who had some idea of the Christian faith but little practice, such as not attending church. These missionaries come with a preconceived idea of what mission is and how these people need to change in order to become faithful

---

18. See Zurlo et al., "World Christianity and Mission 2021." See more on such studies on global mission movements Behera, "Mission in Word—and in Practice?," 81.

19. See more recently, Biehl, "Is Europe Lost?"

20. Kim, *Mission as Process*. The page numbers in the following paragraphs refer to this thesis.

Christians. However, the missionaries' picture of faith and church is deeply Korean, with an emphasis on church planting, discipleship, and evangelism (51). Several authors he quotes, including Kirsteen Kim, confirm that these missionaries' understanding of mission is based on nineteenth-century Western models of mission (26). Their reverse mission is to bring back the gospel they once received and which they feel is fading in the UK.

For our discussion of migrants, mission, and ecumenism, we pick up three aspects of this study. First, the faith journey of the Korean missionaries turns the tables: They came with a solid understanding of mission and evangelism based on what Western missionaries had brought to Korea. Now, with the idea of repaying a debt by bringing back the gospel to Britain, they realize that this concept of mission is not producing results. Second, Kim argues that it is the missionaries who learn and change. They realize that those with whom they engage have made slow progress in their faith, and this fact forces the missionaries to rethink their approach. Kim describes the main impact of the missionary encounter as a change in the missionaries' deep convictions.[21] Third, in the end, his study comes surprisingly close to an empirical confirmation of TTL's position. Faced with the slow progress and realizing that their attempt to integrate believers into congregations is not working well or producing the desired result, the missionaries begin to reflect on a trinitarian *missio Dei* approach that would require to trust less in teaching and more in the Spirit and in discerning faith together. The Korean missionaries support Christians in the UK to take the initiative in their faith journeys; they do not impose anymore their matrix of commitment to a particular church or life-style (195). Instead of attempting to include the Christians they want to win into the existing structures, the congregations should become more flexible in order to be able "to engage with people's faith journeys where they are" (198).

From this story, it appears that these Korean missionaries would agree with the central position of the local congregation in TTL. It can be assumed that they still would question TTL's strong emphasis on the ideal of the local multicultural church as a witness to the diversity of global Christianity. The contours of life they perceive as truly Christian—discipleship as the goal of mission and discipling—would blur the different cultural expressions in the congregation in order to correspond to their original concept of a Christian life.

---

21. Kim described this development using a term borrowed from Zygmund Bauman: liquefaction. See Kim, *Mission as Process*, 14.

REVERSE MISSION?

The highest number of Christian migrants who interpret their mission with reference to the concept of reverse mission, it seems, come to the UK from African countries.[22] Unlike in the case of the Koreans, most of them come from one of the former colonies. This seems to resonate with TTL's statement that the direction of mission has turned. This aspect definitely adds to the complexity of the missionary encounter because the complexities of colonialism "that can manifest itself in racism, discrimination, violence, unfair economic relations between countries and the knowledge that the wealth of the former colonial powers has been acquired at the expense of the colonies" linger on. This past may encourage stereotypes but it also leads to a critique of mission from the West in the past and present.[23]

Israel Oluwole Olofinjana is one theologian who is reflecting on reverse mission in this context. Originally from Nigeria, he is involved in church planting, ministering, and in research in the UK. His reflection is in line with the Korean missionaries' understanding of the contours of what it means to live a truly Christian life. He, however, differs from their concept in reflecting more on the context and the cultural, religious, and even racial diversity he observes in urban parts of the UK. He traces the waves of "black" church planting since 1906 onwards and seeks to develop an African British theology. "As an African theology, African British Theology is a contextual, postcolonial theology which takes into consideration the existential realities of Africans living in a multicultural British society. It relates in this sense to Black British theology, which takes seriously the black experiences of Africans and Caribbean peoples as crucial aspects of theological reflection. This means that African British Theology is a subset of Black British theology. African British theology is also a practical theology which seeks to improve upon the missional practices of African pastors and churches in Britain."[24]

Olofinjana claims that the second task of African British theology is to help African Christians and churches to engage with postmodern secular Britain. This means coming to terms with the fact that the "European worldview no longer accepts God or institutional religion." His missionary

---

22. See Asamoah-Gyadu, "Reverse Evangelism."

23. Nordin and Otterbeck, *Migration and Religion*, 10.

24. He is the founding director of the Centre for Missionaries from the Majority World and serves on the Executive Team of the Lausanne Movement; Olofinjana, *World Christianity in Western Europe*, 193.

impulse is critical of the UK society that is highly secularized, and also critical of the British churches which either seem to fall for secularism or are not working against the decline of religion. This is a dimension of reverse mission, but he also wants to relate his theology to the way in which African Christians are seen by Europeans. Reverse mission "does not only mean reaching out to white British indigenes as if it is a white hunt!" Reverse mission also happens when an African pastor leads an interculturally plural church.[25] This would resonate with TTL's idea of the multicultural diverse local congregation.

It is also intriguing that, without using the term, there are traces of "mission from the margins" in his book. According to Olofinjana reverse mission needs to address deeper "structural issues" of the UK society because these Christians experience "institutional racism," such as lower chances for education which leads to poverty and unemployment. They suffer from regulations on immigration and inequalities in the healthcare system.[26] This is reminiscent of the quoted epistemological privilege people may have because of their marginalization.

Olofinjana's reverse mission not only seeks to change the religious situation or evangelize *white* people. It also addresses the crisis phenomena mentioned in ch. 1. In return, the realities of a society deeply affected by migration are reflected upon from a reverse mission perspective. The majority of Christians he is writing about are joining black churches and not transforming British local churches into multicultural ministries. Reverse mission, too, seems to be mission in crisis.

CROSSING INVISIBLE FRONTIERS

The Korean missionaries Kim interviewed originally planned to bring back the gospel they once have received from Western missionaries. They focus on mission as faith development, as a three-way communication between the missionaries and those they want to evangelize, and each of them with God. Olofinjana offers a wider approach for reverse mission taking greater account of the cultural, social, political, and intercultural aspects of reverse mission in the context of migration.

Migrants not only cross national borders when they enter a country. Their presence makes a multiplicity of hidden frontiers visible. We would

25. Olofinjana, *World Christianity in Western Europe*, 195–96.
26. Olofinjana, *World Christianity in Western Europe*, 196–97.

call them the new multiple ecumenical frontiers: it is a frontier of cultures, of inculturation of the gospel, of languages and theologies, and of different concepts of faith. This approach allows for an examination of the ways in which Christian migrants engage with the Christian faith in the context of the UK, a postmodern, secularized society. It also allows for an investigation of the complexities that arise from the interaction of different layers of belief and practice. In this dynamic situation, the nature and the objective of mission change. It is neither the mission of only the locals nor the mission of only the migrants. TTL's notion of mission as discerning God's presence and the work of the Spirit becomes a helpful concept in this encounter.

Not the least, it is also an ecclesiological frontier. Unlike in the established ecumenical movement, new churches are established by and among migrants and most of them are not concerned about their doctrinal status or confessional tradition. They are concerned about the lives of their members in this world and about the meaning and impact of the Bible on their lives. They come together according to how they live their faith and the ethics that flows from it, and for fellowship and mutual support.[27] This understanding of ecclesiology and Christian life offers a different ground for being church than the traditional ecumenical movement, which essentially seeks to bring together churches that have been splitting over doctrinal and other issues and are now seeking ways to recognize each other as churches of Christ—even if they are not visibly united. The division of the types of churches along "color lines" reflects to some extent the crisis issues that a society "marked by the lingering complexities of colonialism" is going through.[28]

---

27. See for example the description of the self-understanding of African congregations in Biehl, *Is Europe Lost?*, 288–89.

28. Nordin and Otterbeck, *Migration and Religion*, 10.

7

The Missionaries We Need to Envisage

Risto: Marina, you are originally from India, but now you live in the UK working for a Christian academic institution. Do you think that you are an Indian missionary in Europe?

Marina: As a part of my theological education, I was sent by my church to one of its mission fields for a short period. The short stay was an exciting and challenging time but I realized that this way of being in mission is not my vocation.

Risto: Do I hear you saying that mission has many dimensions and you can be involved in many ways? What did you learn during that time?

Marina: I appreciated the encounters I had there and was impressed by the dedication of the missionaries I accompanied. However, I realized how culturally bound this mission endeavor must look to those to whom it reached out. Since then, the question of contextualization has been important to me.

Risto: Now you are no longer working in the Indian culture. Coming from another culture is surely a good basis for your work as theologian in the UK. Do you see yourself as an ambassador of a different way of doing theology?

Marina: I have worked outside of my home region, Mizoram, for the larger part of my life. I worked in theological schools in South India, in Switzerland, and now in the UK. In the European context, I am looked upon as representing the Global South, to bring in a different voice but I feel the interest in changing the way of doing theology here is limited.

The Missionaries We Need to Envisage

Risto: There may be various reasons for that, starting from the dominant culture and a long tradition of doing theology, but changes are always possible, though they may take time. How do you see your role? Would you like to change the way European theologians do theology?

Marina: I see my role as exemplifying how to do theology and to reflect on mission from more than one place, how we can learn to make our theologies interact so that they speak together to a globalized world, and not only to the specific context we come from. This is one reason why I think that in mission we need to look more closely at the communities and not only at individuals.

IN THE WESTERN CONTEXT, we observe much criticism towards mission as being a form of colonialism. Western mission, for example, to the Mizo in northeast India in the nineteenth century happened in a colonial setting. However, research has shown that the indigenous evangelists and Bible women accepted the message from within their tradition, according to what seemed meaningful to them. They developed a contextualized gospel which reached the people.[1] The present-day Presbyterian Church and Baptist Church in Mizoram are missional churches sending out several thousand missionaries, not only to other parts of India but also to other continents—adding to the approximately 430,000 cross-cultural missionaries across the world in 2021.[2] Globally, the Presbyterian Church of Mizoram sends its missionaries in the network of the Council for World Mission.[3] Surprisingly, the present-day Presbyterian Mizo Church seems to promote in its own mission projects in the region[4] in general a model of a culturally (Mizo) bound mission, similar to the one they had been exposed to in its own beginning.[5]

The encounters between those who proclaim and those who appropriate are of significant importance not only to mission studies but also to the reflection on the kind of missionaries we need. The nature of the encounter changes according to the times, the cultural, social, and political settings and the power relations involved. The hyper-complex nature of these processes is one of the reasons why mission is always and everywhere in crisis.

---

1. See Behera, "Mission in Northeast India."
2. Zurlo, "World Christianity and Mission 2021," 16.
3. Council for World Mission, https://www.cwmission.org/.
4. See Mizoram Presbyterian Church, "Synod Mission Board (SMB)."
5. See, for example, Lawmsanga, "Theology of Mission."

No one has full control of the encounter and its inherent tensions. Neither can one know how others interpret what they hear, nor how the proclaimed message will resonate with their lives and contexts over time. Theologically, this can be understood in terms of the work of the Spirit. Contextualization is not merely a process of superficial adaptation, whereby listeners are enabled to assimilate the message more readily.[6] In mission the process of contextualization is inherently open to risk. This raises questions about the assumed success of Western missionaries in the past in their attempts to monitor and control the process. There is substantial evidence from various historical contexts indicating that missionaries were unable to exert complete control. In the case of the Mizo, for example, we find new groups and initiatives springing up, not always to the liking of the missionaries or the colonial officers. In a different context, the story of the so-called African Independent or Instituted Churches (AICs) is another pointer to this risky openness of the missionary process.[7] Sensitive missionaries, often to their own surprise, found that their own faith was transformed as they learned from those among whom they were serving. Often missionaries experienced being transformed by a kind of conversion experience.

In his seminal reflection on mission and theology, *Transforming Mission*, David Bosch gives at least two reasons for the uncertain situation of mission. The fundamental one is that the church knows only one "safe" place, that is at the foot of the cross.[8] The breathtaking vision to witness from the foot of the cross to a cosmic event with consequences for the creation and all humans in it gives the church a direction, but also brings challenges and opposition. The real danger for the church, Bosch argues, is safety and complacency.[9] The second reason is that mission found itself in the second half of the twentieth century in the transition from one mission paradigm to the next emerging one, which he labeled the ecumenical missionary paradigm.[10] The more recent reflection on mission in theological debates resonates well with it being a risky and open encounter.[11] In this

---

6. See Bergmann and Vähäkangas, *Contextual Theology*.

7. Lubaale, "Independents."

8. Bosch, *Transforming Mission*, 519: "The *missio Dei* purifies the church. It sets it under the cross—the only place where it is ever safe. The cross is the place of humiliation and judgement, but it is also the place of refreshment and new birth."

9. Bosch, *Transforming Mission*, 2. A similar argument is advanced by Walls, *Cross-Cultural Process in Christian History*, who makes a statement on the history of the church.

10. Bosch, *Transforming Mission*, 368–89.

11. For the importance of theology for mission and of mission for theology, see, for example, Ross, "Contemporary Ecumenical Missiology."

The Missionaries We Need to Envisage

reflection we can already perceive some of the characteristics of this ecumenical paradigm such as mission from everywhere to everywhere, emphasizing the role of the Spirit instead of the missionary, or the theological confluence among the major recent mission documents, *Together Towards Life* (TTL),[12] the *Cape Town Commitment*[13] of the Lausanne Movement and the Apostolic exhortation *Evangelii Gaudium* of Pope Francis.[14] However, the prevailing critique of mission reminds us that traces and structures of the older "West to the rest" mission model still linger on.

What are the implications of studying experiences from cross-cultural mission in a globalized world characterized by so many different contexts? The perspective adopted here is that of mission studies, rather than that of practitioners engaged in cross-cultural mission work.[15] The aim is to re-conceptualize mission as a risky and open process of negotiation and communication—joining in with the Spirit. In such an approach, the roles of the missionaries and of those addressed by them are transformed. We propose that it is beneficial to conceptualize congregations, rather than individuals, as the primary agents of missionary activity.

MISSION AND MISSIONARIES

In the study process on the occasion of the one hundredth anniversary of the founding of the International Missionary Council (1921–2021),[16] study centers around the world were asked to look for evidence of cooperation in mission in their regions, a task that the authors carried out in different ways.[17] One informative example on issues of cooperation between missionaries comes from China. Missionaries had been sent to the same place by different organizations, and one couple had been warned not to associate with those sent by other organizations. However, once there, they realized in their daily work that they "shared the same motivation for

---

12. Keum, *Together Towards Life*.

13. *Cape Town Commitment*.

14. Pope Francis, *Evangelii Gaudium*. For a comparison of these documents, see for example Bevans, "Transforming Discipleship."

15. See Kim, "Future of Mission Studies," based on the first chapters in Kim, *Oxford Handbook of Mission Studies*.

16. Biehl, "Study Process of the IMC Centenary."

17. See, for example the study by Lalrinthanga, "Cooperation and Unity Among the Mission Churches in Mizoram," 86–88.

service, the same struggles in cross-cultural living, and most importantly the same hopes for their ministries."[18] They developed what the author termed a practical ecumenism distinct from a formal comity agreement as we observe in other regions. The intriguing part of the study is that they developed this ecumenical attitude despite the orders from their sending organizations. The author's main point is that the exigencies of doing cross-cultural mission led to a practical ecumenism and into conflict with the goals of the sending organizations.

Looking at the cross-cultural movement of missionaries and the structures they move in leads to some challenging and unresolved issues in mission. One is the issue of the sending body. It can be argued that William Carey's *Enquiry* (1792) conceptually paved the way for free associations and societies to take on the task of preparing and sending missionaries. This strategic choice also shows the church-critical dimension because in Carey's opinion, the churches of the time neglected their obligation.[19] His approach supported the idea that individuals who feel called to go to other countries are sent by a missionary society to convince non-Christians of the Christian faith and win them over. This example draws attention to some of the structural difficulties and conceptual questions that arise in connection with cross-cultural missionary endeavors and their organization.[20]

In 2017, Michael Stroope produced a critique of mission language ending with the verdict that mission is a very ambiguous and unclear concept and therefore the term should not be used anymore. His extensive critique of the various streams of *missio Dei* theology culminates in adopting Neill's saying: "Missio Dei is everywhere and means everything."[21] The challenge for today, according to Stroope, is that "mission, birthed and developed in the modern age, is itself inadequate language for the church in the current age. Rather than rehabilitating or redeeming mission, we have to move beyond its rhetoric, its practice, and its view of the world."[22]

---

18. Kaiser, "Field Workers and Mission Leaders in Tension."

19. Carey, *Enquiry into the Obligations of Christians*. On the beginnings of modern mission outside the North Atlantic world, see for example Walls, *Cross-Cultural Process in Christian History*.

20. For other challenges of the cross-cultural mission movement see Bendor-Samuel, "Challenge and Realignment," who has a slightly different look at Carey. See also Stanley, "Where Have Our Mission Structures Come From?"

21. Stroope, *Transcending Mission*, 18–19.

22. Stroope, *Transcending Mission*, 26.

The Missionaries We Need to Envisage

The task is therefore not to transform (Bosch), but to transcend mission because "the meaning of mission compounded, and an aggregation of meaning occurred in order to accommodate a variety of agendas and to support a particular version of church history."[23]

We agree that for the emerging ecumenical mission paradigm—to use Bosch's language—we do not only have to transform mission but to transcend its practices and identification with "a particular version of church history" or with the movement of missionaries. In Stroope's critique we find, however, an echo of the learning process of the ecumenical mission movement which transcends such identifications. Stroope describes his own journey as a missionary as having been based on two assumptions: "'Mission is going to people in faraway places to rescue them from eternal damnation' and 'Mission is a calling that only a few can receive.'"[24] Being a missionary in Sri Lanka, he later became uneasy about the colonial legacy that continued to define how mission was understood there. The ambiguity of what the different churches and mission agencies thought mission was and how they practiced it added to his uneasiness.

Stroope's critique points to how structures and concepts from the colonial period continue into the postcolonial period, and these definitely need to be critiqued and transcended. We find such transcending moments in the progress of the ecumenical mission movement that is reflected in its shift from missions(!) to mission.[25] The critiqued ambiguity of mission entered the scene through the move from conceiving of missions—defined by organizations and their strategies such as the spatial approach of Edinburgh 1910—to conceptualizing it as following the traces in the different contexts of God becoming human and of discerning God's presence in creation through the work of the Spirit. One observation on Stroope's book is that in the extensive list of authors reviewed, authors from Asia or more generally from the Global South are missing, with very few exceptions.[26] We are convinced that the transcending happens by opening up to the contextual, multi-dimensional reality and to mission as a risky and open process that includes their voices. Because of this multi-diversity and multi-dimensionality of a messy reality, mission could be understood

---

23. Stroope, *Transcending Mission*, 27.
24. Stroope, *Transcending Mission*, Prologue (Position 116).
25. Crane, "Dropping the S."
26. Exceptions are for example Lamin Sanneh and Ogbu Kalu, Stroope, *Transcending Mission*, 411, 426 passim.

better as a descriptive term for a process than as a clear and tightly defined concept.

MISSION EVERYWHERE

From a theological perspective all missionary approaches share the conviction that a core characteristic of the Christian faith is that it needs to be shared. Many do this in ways that are faithful to the spirit of the gospel. Others adopt aggressive methods while claiming to follow the gospel, sometimes not even recognizing the members of other churches as Christians and proselytizing them. Even within the Christian spectrum, mission continues to be a contested process. Looking around the globe today, there is great diversity in terms of the forms of mission being practiced. We see mission organizations, several of them today based in the Global South.[27] We find migrant or international congregations engaging in mission in many centers in the heartland of former Christendom. But most of all, we see today more clearly the mission of churches in the Global South whose existence precedes Western missionary efforts. We also see new independent mission efforts in many of the provinces of world Christianity. We see house churches, small fellowships, insider movements,[28] and many other forms of being church and engaging in mission. Then there are countless reports of people coming to faith in Jesus Christ after having experienced healing and miracles of all kinds. Others report visions, dreams, and prophecies which we can attribute to the work of the Holy Spirit, not to the conscious attempt of any missionary.[29] This panorama shows that mission today is happening everywhere in many forms, and what is more, encompasses movements from everywhere to everywhere, thus transcending the colonial pattern of an allegedly Christian and a non-Christian world. All this is happening in a postcolonial world in very diverse constellations. To look at all of it only from the perspective of Western mission's past in a colonial setting is to deny the plurality of mission today and to deny agency to a huge group of people.

---

27. See, for example, Gospel for Asia (GFA) (Gospelforasia.org); OMF International (ofm.org); Operation Mobilisation (OM) (om.org).

28. See, for example, the movement of Yesu Bhaktas, described by Bhakiaraj, "Christianity in South-Central Asia, 1910–2010," 142.

29. Kim, *Joining in with the Spirit*.

The Missionaries We Need to Envisage

We do not agree with all that is happening globally under the term mission and some forms call for serious criticism. The document *Christian Witness in a Multi-Religious World* is a response to the kind of aggressive and denigrating practices people of other or no faith have suffered and continue to experience from Christian missionaries, such as the destruction of places of worship or sacred texts, exploitation of vulnerabilities, and bearing false witness against other religions. Such behavior is contradicting authentic Christian witness as it is expounded in this milestone document.[30]

In today's globalized world, the sharing of experiences and self-critical reflections interact across national and cultural frontiers. In this interaction one realizes that mission is not identical with a strategy of converting the other, but that it relates to the whole church, its life and expressions in a given context. It also relates to its catholicity and the question of unity. One of the important steps in the global reflection on mission has therefore been the shift to mission as a dimension of the life of the church. Every aspect and each activity of the church participates in mission because God is involving it in God's mission.

The multi-dimensional character of mission is reflected in how mission studies are placed within the canons of theology. In some it is placed under practical theology as doing mission, while some consider it as a translateral dimension which can be studied in church history, biblical studies, or in the relation to other faiths. And others highlight it as the core of theology such as *missio Dei* speaking of God as a missionary God.[31]

MISSION IN *TOGETHER TOWARDS LIFE*

Can traces of such historical and contextual experiences and of such debates be identified in recent mission statements? In TTL, one thread of the argument is about ecumenism and mission. Paragraph 65 speaks of the Commission on World Mission and Evangelism (CWME) as the heir of the International Missionary Council. The paragraph explains that the churches in the fellowship of the World Council of Churches (WCC) brought their understanding of mission and unity to bear on the discussions of the CWME and cooperated in it with the Roman Catholic Church. The Lausanne Movement for World Evangelization and the World Evangelical

---

30. *Christian Witness in a Multi-Religious World*, Principles 5 and 6. The issues listed here are quoted in Keum, *Together Towards Life*, §90.

31. Behera, "Mission."

Alliance (WEA) are also listed as having "abundantly contributed to the enrichment of ecumenical theological reflection on mission in unity." The common concern is "that the whole church should witness to the whole gospel in the whole world" (TTL, §65). This certainly is one aspect of the new ecumenical missionary paradigm that Bosch saw dawning in the last century.[32]

The passages in TTL that speak of ecumenical mission declare that the credibility of mission depends on the ability to speak with one voice. Many churches have, through long dialogues, come to reconciliation over the conflicts that separated them, restoring forms of unity, and some even uniting. However, while visible unity is important, for mission it is more important "to discern what helps the cause of God's mission. In other words, unity in mission is the basis for the visible unity of the churches which also has implications for the order of the church" (TTL, §69).

In continuing the *missio Dei* line of reasoning, TTL emphasizes the Spirit as the missionary. The task of Christians is therefore not to bring God to a situation where God is absent but, rather, "to witness to the God who is already there" (TTL, §94). This approach of the *missio Spiritus*[33] has an important consequence. The focus of TTL is not on the figure of the missionary as the agent of mission, but on the church joining in the work of the Spirit. In TTL "missionary" is an adjective which is used to characterize God (TTL, §2), activities, or the missionary movement (TTL, §26, §49)—and the churches which need to be missionary churches (TTL, §58). In TTL, missionaries are mentioned only once, as figures of the past (TTL, §87).

TTL locates the missionary task mainly and foremost in the local congregations. The section on the local congregations precedes the section on evangelism and makes thus the congregation the locus of a missionary spirituality and of activities which can be considered to be evangelism in the sense of an "explicit and intentional articulation of the gospel" (TTL, §85). Whereas in the past missionaries crossed the sea, "more than ever before, local congregations today can play a key role in emphasizing the crossing of cultural and racial boundaries and affirming cultural difference as a gift of the Spirit" (TTL, §75) and "can also, as never before, develop global connections" (TTL, §76).

---

32. Bosch, *Transforming Mission*, 368.
33. See Kim, *Joining in with the Spirit*; Yong, "Primed for the Spirit."

For TTL, the local congregation is the prime location for an authentic discipleship. "Authentic evangelism is grounded in humility and respect for all, and flourishes in the context of dialogue. . . . Such authentic relationships are often best nourished in local faith communities, and based on local cultural contexts. Christian witness is as much by our presence as by our words" (TTL, §89). The section on the local congregation should probably be read in the light of the preceding passages on mission in unity. It is, however, surprising that TTL's section on the local congregations is inward looking; the reality of local congregations of different denominations next to each other in the same space is not discussed as a dimension of mission or as a question to unity. In that section any mention of an ecumenical witness of local congregations which exist in the same neighborhood is conspicuously absent.

BEING A MISSIONARY AND BEING MISSIONARY

The relevant passages of TTL already give a good impression of the local congregations as missionary communities and how they can transform to become interculturally open communities. Confirming that the basis for mission is the presence of the missionary God in the Holy Spirit, we can add that today we find forms of Christian presence in almost all countries.[34] When we understand mission primarily as the mission of God, enacted through the presence and action of the Holy Spirit, questions arise about conceptions that depend heavily on human activity. We are critical of strategic plans such as identifying "unreached peoples," "finishing the task," or concepts like the 10/40 window, requesting to concentrate activities in space between the 10 degree north and 40 degree north latitude.[35] We discern traces of the older spatial approach in which it is the task of well-equipped organizations to allocate their resources led by such strategies.[36] Some of such thinking is still reflected in statistical approaches such as calculating the number of Great Commission Christians in the *Atlas of Global Christianity* or in questions such as are asked by the *World Christian*

---

34. See for example, the series "Edinburgh Companions to Global Christianity" mapping the diverse regions of Christianity; https://edinburghuniversitypress.com/.

35. See, for example, Joshua Project, "What Is the 10/40 Window?"

36. See Bendor-Samuel's critique in the same line, in his "Challenge and Realignment," 271.

Encyclopedia project as to how many people still lack access to the Christian message.[37]

Mission is first of all the work of the Spirit, emphasizing that God in the Spirit is everywhere before "we" come as missionaries. In humility and faith, we recognize that the "Spirit works in the world often in mysterious and unknown ways beyond our imagination" (TTL, §15). This conviction is hopeful and prompts us to trust and expect to encounter the presence and action of the Holy Spirit in every context. TTL and the "Arusha Call" emphasize the concept of mission from the margins: "We are called to joyfully engage in the ways of the Holy Spirit, who empowers people from the margins with agency, in the search for justice and dignity."[38] Mission in the Spirit means to trust that the Spirit finds a way to the people. The *missio Spiritus*[39] approach affects how we theologize about people who do not know Christ. We are aware that this is a controversial issue, particularly between the different traditions in the mission movement.

Accepting the presence of God in the action of God's Spirit everywhere has great significance for our understanding of mission. The accompanying spirituality is compassionate but serene because of the primordial role of the Spirit in mission. In this perspective, it is important to redefine the possible relationship between the individual missionaries, the agencies they work with, and the church. In addition to missionaries, in today's global and digitally connected world, there are so many ways of hearing the gospel and being involved in a fellowship such as radio and television programs, websites, and other media. Diaspora communities too can share the faith back to their countries of origin. There needs to be renewed reflection on the authority of mission, the relationship between vocation and mission, and the responsibility of sending and being sent in relation to the fellowship of churches.

Against this background, the attitude to mission which congregations and communities should develop could be characterized on the basis of the signs of the church: *kerygma, leiturgia, martyria, diaconia*. They characterize according to ecumenical theology, a church, but in the perspective of Bosch's distinction between an intentional and a dimensional level of

---

37. Johnson and Ross, *Atlas of Global Christianity*, 290–93; Zurlo, "World Christianity and Mission," 17. See, for example, the discussion on Frontier Mission in: Snodderly and Moreau, *Evangelical and Frontier Mission*.

38. "Arusha Call to Discipleship," 3.

39. See Yong, "Primed for the Spirit."

mission, they can easily be translated into a missional language: proclamation, missional spirituality, witness, serving the people "and healing as wholeness and reconciliation into koinonia—communion with God, communion with people, and communion with creation as a whole."[40] The signs of the church become the signs of missional congregations as they have already been described at the World Mission Conference in Salvador de Bahia (1996). The participants identified competitiveness among churches and evangelism that does not respect the culture of the people as not reflecting "the gracious love of God and the challenge of the gospel." Instead: "Local congregations are called to be places of hope, providing spaces of safety and trust wherein different peoples can be embraced and affirmed, thus manifesting the inclusive love of God. For congregations in increasingly plural societies, inclusion of all cultural groups which make up the community, including those who are uprooted, marginalised, and despised is important. Strengthening congregations through a spirituality which enables them to face the vulnerability involved in this openness is critical."[41]

This concept can be enriched by connecting it with the Athens World Mission Conference (2005) that promoted the concept of the congregations as hospitable spaces of healing and reconciliation in the Holy Spirit whose light radiates to those around them.[42]

This reflection, harvesting the ecumenical debate on mission of the last decades, leads us to characterize missional congregations by these signs:

- They live a spirituality of hospitality which is a witness to the trinitarian communion of God.
- They cultivate an attitude of patient listening instead of emphasizing to convince.[43]
- They cultivate a lifestyle of witnessing as an adequate way of proclaiming.
- In their encounter with people, they adopt an attitude of prophetic dialogue.[44]

---

40. "Mission and Evangelism in Unity Today," 63–64.
41. Duraisingh, *Called to One Hope*, 24.
42. Matthey, *"Come, Holy Spirit, Heal and Reconcile!"*
43. Robert Schreiter observes that mission today entails listening before speaking, contemplating before acting, in: Kalu, *Mission after Christendom*, 15.
44. See Bevans and Schroeder, *Prophetic Dialogue*.

Such congregations open up to new and creative ways of theology and faith, engaging with the changing world in which they live and with the future, not the trodden paths of the past. They can realize unity in and through mission, in the interrelation with churches of other traditions at the same location and at other places which defines the ecumenical quality of a church.

AND THE MISSIONARY VOCATION?

In the new paradigm of ecumenical mission(al) theology, the priority is with the local congregations and churches. This calls for new models to explain how cross-cultural missionaries can enrich the church's mission. Bendor-Samuel proposes in his discussion of this relationship to hear the great command "to go" of Matt 28 not without the invitation "to come (over)" (Acts 17).[45] This establishes a relational mutuality in the agency in mission. For this to take effect, the role of missionaries will need to be defined by the ecumenical mission within the fellowship of churches in mission, instead of letting mission be defined by the concept of the missionary. Within this new framework we can still expect that people will be inspired by a missionary vocation, as they have been throughout history. Among the surprises of the Spirit is the calling of individuals to offer a witness of sacrifice, solidarity, and service—whether far from home or near.

This paradigm, in addition, brings to bear two core principles from the Reformation tradition on mission. Firstly, it expands the concept of the priesthood of all believers to mission, emphasizing the entire church community's role in witnessing, rather than relegating mission only to specialists known as missionaries. Secondly, it recognizes the multifaceted nature of mission today, valuing the specialized knowledge of believers in diverse fields. Their breadth of expertise, from ecology and economics to peace studies and conflict resolution, poverty alleviation, education, sciences, and gender issues and many more, is essential for the church as part of its mission to effectively address the multiple crises mentioned at the outset of this book. By harnessing this wide range of expertise, the church is better equipped to "be prepared to give an answer to everyone who asks you to give the reason for the hope that you have. But do this with gentleness and respect" (1 Pet 3:15), a hope that refers to the breathtaking vision of God's mission for God's creation in which God invites us to join.

45. See Bendor-Samuel, "Challenge and Realignment," 275–76.

8

The Formation We Need to Offer

Kenneth: Why is theological education important for you?

Michael: Theological education works at the intersection of the past, the present, and the future. What do we learn from previous generations—and what do we need to un-learn—what can we add to knowledge and theology. What will we be able to pass on through teaching and learning with the future generation. It is also crucial for how we address issues of a contextual relevant theology.

Kenneth: How have you been involved?

Michael: I had the opportunity to do my own theological and religious studies in different countries and since then I have been fascinated by the different ways of doing theology and by teaching. I was trained and worked as pastor. Later I taught at university level and accompanied doctoral students. Through most of my professional life I engaged with teachers, doctoral students, and those responsible for theological education, mainly in what we call the Global South. With them I learned a lot about doing theology.

Kenneth: What about mission formation?

Michael: From the perspective of missio Dei *theology*, mission is an integral dimension of the church's life. Theology, therefore, has a missional dimension, and it naturally needs to critically study its history in mission. We also need to be aware that we do our theology in a choir of different voices, each with a distinctive theological understanding. This is the ecumenical dimension, which is equally important for how we do theology.

EDUCATION IN MISSION

IT IS A CONTROVERSIAL question how the term "mission" relates to the Bible. Some claim that the Bible is the story of God's mission, while others question this interpretation.¹ In the search for a biblical basis for mission, Matt 28 plays an important role. It is part of the process of decolonizing mission and its theologies to recognize that the importance given to Matt 28 has to do with its selection by agents in mission from the eighteenth century onwards. By this choice they promoted two related claims: that the task at hand was to convert "heathens" beyond the North Atlantic world, and that the responsibility for this task had to be taken up by free associations of Christians, because the churches of the region did not see it as their responsibility.² In Matt 28:19, however, we find the aspect of teaching. The translation of *matheteusate* as making disciples comes from the Latin translation *discipuli*, meaning students.³ Those who became followers of Jesus were understood to be learners (disciples), and from the early church's time onwards, there has been an emphasis on education, as evidenced by the catechumenate. This aspect of learning and teaching has also accompanied the church in the form of the question about the relation of reason and faith.

In Europe, one dimension of the Reformation was to bring about an educational revolution, and this shaped the churches that emerged from it. In the modern missionary movement, schools were seen as one of the privileged places for proclaiming the good news by enabling future Christians to read the Bible. Schools, however, were not only for Bible study, but also for education in the sciences and humanities, in which the West thought itself superior to anything the "heathens" could produce.⁴ This combination exposed the modern missionary movement to the criticism

---

1. Nguyên, "Mission and Biblical Studies" defends an understanding of the Bible as the story of God's mission while, for example, Stroope, *Transcending Mission*, heavily criticizes this interpretation. For a classic study on mission and the Bible see Bosch, *Transforming Mission*, 15–178.

2. See the argumentation of Carey, *Enquiry into the Obligations of Christians;* and of Warneck, *Evangelische Missionslehre*. Such claims are still upheld by the distinct category of *Great Commission Christians* in Johnson and Ross, *Atlas of Global Christianity*, 290–93.

3. Reinbold, "Gehet hin und machet zu Jüngern alle Völker!?"

4. The participants of the 1910 Edinburgh conference, however, identified the growing risk that the "modern secular education" promoted by governments, would leave "the rising generation practically without religion." *Carrying the Gospel to All the Non-Christian World*, 29.

that, in the colonial era, conversion to the Christian faith was in various regions simultaneously conceived as a progression from primitivism to civilization. The Nigerian church historian Ogbu Kalu is not alone in recognizing that the missionary societies' goal of spreading the gospel in Africa and Asia through local teachers and evangelists was made part of a civilizing mission. In looking back at the World Missionary Conference at Edinburgh in 1910, he observed that in the educational institutions they established, Western models were introduced with the aim of achieving a moral re-education as part of such a civilizing mission. According to him the education offered by mission in that period in Africa was in principle and above all vocational training,[5] not an education according to Humboldt's humanistic ideal of which the Europeans were so proud. If we claim today to decolonize theological education, we need therefore to not only consider the ideals of education but the practices and the tacit underlying assumptions about the knowledge it imparts.

With Matt 28, the mission movement focused on the role of missionaries and their teaching. At the World Missionary Conference Edinburgh 1910, the training of indigenous and autochthonous Christian church leaders was discussed. The report of commission III was titled "Education in Relation to the Christianisation of National Life."

> We wish to lay it down that we believe that the primary purpose to be served by the educational work of missionaries is that of training the native Church to bear its own proper witness. And insomuch as the only way in which the native Church can bear its own proper witness, and can move forward towards the position of independence and self-government in which it ought to stand, is through native leaders, teachers, and officers, we believe that the most important of all the ends which missionary education ought to set itself to serve, is that of training those who are to be the spiritual leaders and teachers of the men of their own nation.[6]

The International Missionary Council introduced the Theological Education Fund in 1958 which was integrated into the World Council of Churches (WCC) in 1976. This fund continued through various stages, accompanying theological education and emphasizing the urgent need for theological education and formation.[7]

---

5. Kalu, "To Hang a Ladder in the Air."
6. *Education in Relation to the Christianisation of National Life*, 371–72.
7. Kaunda, "Imagining a Just and Equitable African Christian Community."

THEOLOGICAL EDUCATION IN THE ECUMENICAL MOVEMENT

So far, theological education has been approached from within the missionary movement, focusing on educating indigenous clergy and neglecting the discussion on the education of the missionary. Even after the shift from missions to mission, some continue to refer to mission as a particular activity, but in the ecumenical movement it is now understood as a dimension of the church expressed in proclamation (*kerygma*), prayer, worship and the celebration of the inviting community (*leiturgia*), service (*diaconia*), and witness (*martyria*), thus paralleling the signs of the church.[8] This leads to affirmations that can also be found in *Together Towards Life* (TTL): Without mission, the church is not a church (TTL, §57). From this perspective, we can say that theological education is missional by nature, reflecting on the relationship between God and God's creatures (and creation), on the Bible, on the existence of the church in history and its present, discerning and teaching how to read the world in the light of the gospel and how to witness and to serve the world. This missional perspective fits into a broad definition of theological education and formation. In the smallest house church or fellowship, forms of theological education are offered as an integral part of discipling and community building, and it can be seen in the desire of their leaders for training. It ranges from here through Bible schools, seminaries and colleges to secular universities with theological faculties. Theological education is for all members of the church. Some are trained as the personnel the church needs to serve its members and the society in various capacities. Others are educated to fulfill their roles in society and their professional lives with a Christian perspective; and all are formed to grow in faith and to live their lives responsibly as Christians. The aim of theological education is to empower the whole church to fulfill its mission to proclaim and serve the world at different levels and in a variety of ministries.

Theological education was prominent at the WCC assembly in Busan in 2013. In 2011–2013, several organizations had conducted a "Global Survey on Theological Education" to be presented in Busan. One of the findings was the continuing lack of availability of theological education, particularly in regions where Christianity has been growing rapidly.[9] Participants in an

---

8. "Mission and Evangelism in Unity Today," §7.

9. *Global Survey on Theological Education*, "Summary of Main Findings." Assuming a

Ecumenical Conversation on ecumenical formation and theological education at the assembly noted that this lack contrasted sharply with the crucial significance of education and formation for the future of the church. Addressing ecumenical issues in education was seen as fundamental for the unity of the church, and an adequate education and formation accessible for all in order for churches to become just and inclusive communities was seen as imperative. In order to achieve these goals, it was said that the different traditions needed to be represented in the student and faculty bodies and their perspectives needed to be included in the curriculum.[10]

The continuing importance and global interest in theological education and formation is demonstrated by a large body of studies in the various regions of world Christianity.[11] Initiatives such as the *Global Forum of Theological Educators*, which brings together people from all Christian traditions in analogy to the *Global Christian Forum*, show that pedagogical, didactic, and methodological issues as well as quality standards for theological education make this area a good platform for dialogue across traditional ecumenical divides.[12]

Theological education, particularly ecumenical education, aims at strengthening the churches in their capacity to communicate the gospel contextually and interculturally and to work together in mission and unity globally. It enables them to respond in a theologically responsible way to the opportunities and challenges of their respective contexts and to the implications of global challenges, and to have a transforming impact in societies for compassion, justice, peace, and the integrity of creation. These far-reaching goals can only be achieved if they are accompanied by the formation of Christian individuals who bear authentic witness to the gospel. Theological education is formation in spirituality and witnessing, not just acquiring knowledge about God, the world, and how to communicate it. In a narrower sense, theological education means the formation

---

correlation between the importance attributed to theological education and the willingness to respond to a survey, one wonders why significantly less Lutherans, Methodists, and Catholics responded to the survey—traditions normally alert to the importance of theology and learning.

10. Senturias and Gill, *Encountering the God of Life*, 167–69.

11. See Werner et al., *Handbook of Theological Education in World Christianity*; Phiri and Werner, *African Handbook on Theological Education*; Antone, *Asian Handbook on Theological Education and Ecumenism*; Kalaitzidis, *Orthodox Handbook for Teaching Ecumenism*; Werner, *Training to Be Ministers in Asia*.

12. Kern and Ruiz, "Global Forum of Theological Educators."

of theologians and other professionals—deacons, religious educators, educators, and specialists—needed by the churches to respond responsibly to the mark of the church—*leiturgia* and *kerygma*—and to serve people and societies through *martyria* and *diaconia*.

It is no exaggeration to say that the major global ecumenical fellowships and organizations agree in principle that theological education plays a crucial role for the future of the churches in this world in crisis. A 2012 global study report of the *World Conference of Associated Theological Institutions* (WOCATI) identified a crisis scenario: the world is in crisis, dramatic changes in world Christianity lead the global fellowship and ecumenism into crisis, and theological education is in crisis. "Some would speak of an emerging global crisis in theological education which are becoming obvious increasingly and will be marking the next decades in the twenty-first century having the potential of endangering the very future and integrity of world Christianity. Others would speak of major challenges for theological education in the period immediately ahead."[13]

It seems to us that not much has changed since then, the plenary on missional formation at the World Mission Conference in Arusha (2018) having echoed this analysis.[14]

WHAT WE NEED

We situate our reflections on the formation and education we need to offer within the framework of world Christianity. This is broader than that of the ecumenical movement, which is largely defined by the relationship of churches based on doctrinal dialogues and formal agreements. In the context of world Christianity, the depth of the crisis scenarios and the scope of the transformation to be achieved by well-educated actors correlate in a revealing way with the comprehensive expectations of those who conceive or demand theological education.[15] It should disciple Christians, form them spiritually and help them to grow in faith, assist them to mature into prophets of justice and apostles of peace, and empower them for mission as critical contemporaries. It should support local congregations in becoming healing and reconciling communities,[16] and should transform

13. *World Report on the Future of Theological Education in the 21st Century*, 53.
14. "Missional Formation," 147–72.
15. For what follows, refer also to *In Gottes Lehre*.
16. Matthey, *"Come, Holy Spirit, Heal and Reconcile!"*

them into spaces transcending the "cultural and racial boundaries, and affirming cultural difference as a gift of the Spirit."[17] It should critically reflect on truth and enable people to proclaim the word of God in multicultural and multi-religious contexts with an attitude of respect.[18] It should critically safeguard and transmit the body of knowledge of its own tradition and develop further awareness of global Christianity for future generations. It should provide training in confessional traditions and promote ecumenical dialogue to overcome fragmentation. It should familiarize people with the richness of theological thought and assist them in their transforming discipleship and their service to the world,[19] including dialoguing with secular disciplines at university level.

In order to respond to these high expectations, we need quality theological education and formation, ranging from the training and equipping of church members, volunteers, and church leaders to the education of specialist theologians. A leading concept for this broad approach is the priesthood of all believers, which, following the idea of the congregations as a community of learning, confessing, and celebrating believers, emphasizes the training and spiritual formation of all church members. Another important concept in this broad understanding is that of lifelong learning. What is important here is not only the ability of churches to provide and offer such programs for different groups, but also to relate them to each other and to integrate them into an overarching concept.

In today's age of global Christianity, it is imperative that such concepts support the catholicity of the church and the consciousness of global Christianity as *oikoumene*, the whole inhabited world. By ecumenical we mean being able to relate one's own ecclesial and theological tradition to others' and engaging with the issues of world Christianity and the ecumenical movement with a priority on those relevant for each particular context and service. As a minimum, it means that educational and training institutions should conceive of their programs in relation to the wider reality of a global Christianity. To be ecumenical in such a way means to be convinced of one's own truth and the validity of practicing one's faith without claiming that this form is exhausting God's will.

This can be understood as an implementation of the well-known San Antonio formula on the relation of the Christian faith to other faiths: "We

---

17. Keum, *Together Towards Life*, §75.
18. *Christian Witness in a Multi-Religious World*.
19. "Missional Formation."

cannot point to any other way of salvation than Jesus Christ; at the same time we cannot set limits to the saving power of God."[20] It actually alludes to an intra-trinitarian dynamic. It is the same triune God, Creator of the world, whose love is shown in the Son, who is the way, the truth and the life, and who works and blows in his world as the Spirit. Whereas in San Antonio the formula was meant to reconcile, in a conflict about the priority in mission, Christians can adopt both attitudes without making them contradictory. Transformed by God's love, we owe the message of God's love to all and we proclaim it as we have experienced it. Here, as disciples we are exclusivists. However, in order to remain faithful to our God, we go forth, cross borders and discern the Spirit from the spirits and we will be able to find traces of God in the lives of faith and witness of others, thus being inclusive and learning together. An analogical ecumenical positionality should inform ecumenical theological education: we need to be discerning in relation to the tradition in which we are rooted while being inclusive and even open to plurality in joining in the *missio Dei*.

Missional Formation and Discipleship

The aspects of mission in a world in crisis are part of the content and object of theological reflection and formation. The believers and their churches can, together with other actors, contribute to resolving these crises by searching for responses in faith. Such formation is not only about knowledge and skills, but also about spirituality and lives lived as Christian. The history of the ecumenical movement offers a rich tradition and the worldwide Christian fellowship is the resonance body for the sharing of experiences, insights and arguments in addressing the crises. This applies to theological education, too.

Without being able to go into this in depth here, we can look at the early Christian congregations as communities of confessing learners. Paul describes himself in his first letter as a follower of Christ. In 1 Thess 1:6, he understands discipleship as imitating the example of Jesus (*imitatio*): "And you became imitators of us and of the Lord, for in spite of persecution you received the word with joy inspired by the Holy Spirit." In the later Corinthian correspondence (1 Cor 11:1), Paul urges his readers to "follow my example, as I follow the example of Christ," whereby "follow my example" translates *mimethai*, i.e., imitate. The concept of *imitatio* and the

---

20. Wilson, *San Antonio Report*, 32.

practice associated with it had and continue to have considerable influence in church history and theology.

Today, we need to figure out what following Jesus's example and becoming Christ-like can look like in the different contexts of a globally interconnected world. The contributions to the plenary session on "Missional Education" during the last World Mission Conference in Arusha in 2018 provide an example. The panelists understood education as a practice of discipleship aimed at transforming the world. In this context, the term "counter-culture" is used. Christians should live in the world without being shaped by the world. This emphasizes the spiritual dimension of life and calls for a changed lifestyle as a witness. On the panel, the mission scholar Kirsteen Kim criticized the fact that in seminaries and training centers, especially those of the historic churches, too much energy is spent on learning the tradition of one's own denomination in order to be able to carry it on.[21]

An advantage of the proposed broad approach to formation and lifelong learning is that different ways of doing theology can be related to each other, depending on the target groups, the context, and objectives. A more experiential, spiritual, and group-based formation can be very conducive for certain purposes and stages and is widely used in models of ecumenical or global learning. It can be argued that non-formal theological education programs for adults, such as Theological Education at Extension (TEE), owe their origins primarily to a critical stance towards a university-based education, which is accessible to few in the Global South. They have been particularly influenced by emancipatory movements since the 1960s, by pedagogies such as those of Paulo Freire, and of social science theories of lifelong learning, development, and processes of social change.[22] Such approaches can also be useful for academically trained theologians who are more accustomed to working with texts and theories. A wisdom-oriented theology can enter into dialogue with a research-oriented theology or an intercultural reading of the Bible as it can be practiced by Bible study groups and congregations.[23] One of the remarkable resources of the church is that it is one of the very few social institutions that can offer different places

---

21. "Panel Interview with Kwabena Asamoah-Gyadu, Kirsteen Kim, and Youhanon Mar Demetrios," 156.

22. Ott, *Beyond Fragmentation*, 222–27. See Kinsler, *Diversified Theological Education*.

23. Compare, for example, exciting studies such as De Wit, *Reading Through the Eyes of Another*.

with different forms of learning. This corresponds well with the diversity of its people, their gifts, and needs.[24]

Education in a Contextual and Global Perspective

Another way of approaching education as ecumenical and missional is to focus on how education and formation contribute to negotiating contextual and global perspectives.[25] The high expectations for education can also be read as an indicator of the points of pain in world Christianity when it comes to ecumenism, mission, unity, and service. Theological education in the context of world Christianity needs to evolve in response to changing global dynamics, cultural shifts, and technological advancements. Theological institutions need to continue incorporating a more diverse and global curriculum. This includes the integration of perspectives from different regions, cultures, and theological traditions to prepare for a more interconnected world. Theological education needs to be intercultural and interdisciplinary and that means enabling people to dialogue with other disciplines from a theological and missional perspective. This does not mean, however, to add more and more issues. We do not need theologians to be the better economists or experts in environmental and climate-related questions; we need those who are able to engage with experts in the related fields from a theological perspective.

Who could be better placed to address global challenges and their impact on local contexts than a global community sharing a common worldview of a God who continues to be present and active in creation? It has to be said, however, that when it comes to assessing the state of theological education, it is definitely less organized, interrelated, and supported than international cooperation among development agencies. Like a *basso continuo*, reports and studies on the situation of theological education institutions in the Global South are underpinned by complaints about their precarious financial situation, the lack of well-trained teachers, the deplorable state of libraries, the lack of good theological literature in the relevant languages. We join in this lament but argue that one problem is that much of what is there in different contexts is not known elsewhere and does not catch the attention in the Western academia.

---

24. See also Singh and Farr, *Christianity and Education*.
25. See, for example, Schreiter, *New Catholicity*.

The Formation We Need to Offer

We find researchers in universities in the Global North building their academic careers on studies on groups and phenomena in the Global South. Particularly in theology we need more researchers from other regions of world Christianity to be involved in the study of phenomena in the Global North—if they are interested. In the area of research and the development of foundational theological literature, we need to see more networking and mutual support, also in addressing the crises of our times. Regions and churches, in their diversity, depend on each other in critical solidarity, also in education and research. Here too, we see promising models and good approaches, not least the IMC study process.

Decolonization of Theology

One process accompanying the negotiation of the global and the local is decolonizing theological education. Decolonizing theological education and challenging Eurocentric and colonial biases in theological thought is a critical endeavor to make theological studies more inclusive, diverse, and relevant. It is an ongoing process that requires commitment, dialogue, critical discernment, and a willingness to transform. Many indigenous and local theological movements have emerged in response to colonialism and globalization, each with its own unique perspective and contribution. Theological institutions can take significant steps toward challenging Eurocentric and colonial biases, creating a more inclusive education. Such steps include reexamination of the curricula and reevaluation of the canon of theological texts to include writings from non-Western perspectives, indigenous cultures, and marginalized communities. But it is not only about inclusion of voices, it is about reevaluating epistemic assumptions by using postcolonial approaches, of liberation and indigenous theologies.[26]

Theological institutions in the fellowship of churches can ensure that they have diverse faculty and students who represent the variety of cultural, ethnic, and theological backgrounds. Such diversity will provide multiple perspectives and challenge Eurocentric biases. Theologically, decolonization can be strengthened by seeing the world and people in the light of the gospel and by offering the perspective of seeing, judging, and acting in order to free the gospel and church from imprisonment in the dominant culture.

---

26. "World Christianity as Post-Colonialising of Theology," in Bergmann and Vähäkangas, *Contextual Theology*, 221–37.

Digital / Online Education

Digital or online education is not new in the field of theological education. The increasing digitization of the world and the pressures of regulating life during the pandemic have meant that even less well-equipped or prepared schools have taken education to the digitized space. In many cases, this was an attempt to use digital technology in order to continue teaching as it took place in classrooms before the pandemic. However, through this experience, many schools have at least moved closer to a hybrid model of education and have developed their capacity to deliver education digitally and online.[27] While there is still a significant digital divide, something significant has happened because few would want to return to pre-pandemic level without online elements in learning and teaching. To speak of a post-digital world, a world that cannot go back to the pre-digital age, is also supported by the fact that in many communities, including in the Global South, community and church life has been organized through digital platforms during the pandemic. This has opened up access to churches and Christian life for new groups, changed the behavior of church members and multiplied forms of communication.[28]

The communiqué of a conference held in Ghana in 2022, organized by major world fellowships, proposed to reconfigure the assumed gap between learning in proximity—said to be physical—and virtual. It highlighted that online spaces are a

> "holy ground" of encounter with God and one another. A theology of hospitality can remind us of the need to make space for one another and for God's presence among us in whichever medium, and of the porous and temporary nature of the roles of host and visitor, instructor and learner. It can ground us in a eucharistic and liturgical theology as it draws our attention back to Christ as the host and the bread of theological education in whichever space. It encourages us to recognize that just like in other liturgical spaces, our transitory attendance of online and offline spaces of theological education is also to edify and commission, nourish and send us into the world.[29]

---

27. This has been discussed in an international and ecumenical conference in December 2022, organized by the World Communion of Reformed Churches, WCC, Lutheran World Federation and EMW. See *Pandemic and Pedagogy*.

28. Campbell, *Distanced Church*.

29. *Pandemic and Pedagogy*, 4.

The communiqué also offers diaspora as an analytical category to discern the "modes of physical and intellectual dislocation and relocation. Just like residential learning, online learning decontextualizes and decenters, albeit in different ways. Models of blended and multi-modal learning, which combine phases of physical co-presence with remote/online phases as well as a variety of media/tion, are best poised to negotiate the distinct challenges of both modalities, build intentional community, sustain it over time and space, and allow for transcultural as well as contextual immersion."[30]

Online or digital formation, therefore, can be contextual. It challenges formation to include the skills of using digital media and must also include, at least in the area of research, the resonance and feedback of these changes on the understanding of the church and on the practices of church life. Digital-based education offers new opportunities for the future of theological education but needs to address again strategies for equitable resource sharing and collaboration between institutions on both sides of the digital gap.

A WAY FORWARD

At many places in the world, we still find the following model of theological education. A church has an explicit idea of what its future clergy need to learn. This includes a canon of basic theological knowledge, the denominational history and profile, as well as skills that are to be acquired through studies, for example, to translate theological issues into language that is understandable for the congregation and for the community and the public. The requirements lead to a curriculum that is implemented in a seminary or at a university. Professors teach young students who are prepared to embark on this long journey and to become ministers of this church after their studies. Their suitability for this is determined in examinations, and their success is attested with a certificate.[31]

Financially and structurally, this model is sustainable only for rich churches. Against the background of the fragility of theological educational institutions, we need a theological education that transcends this type of formation and that can be offered as ecumenical, interdisciplinary, and diverse by various institutions at different places. We see signs of such renewed models in many places and some in places where the scarcity of

---

30. *Pandemic and Pedagogy*, 5.
31. As background to this, see *In Gottes Lehre*.

resources requests creativity and encourages ecumenical cooperation. One of the challenges for the future is to identify new creative models, connect them, and have them interact with the more formal type of education.

9

The Complacency We Need to Explode

Risto: Michael, you have had several important functions as a theologian and you have contributed to the ecumenical movement in many ways over many years. What has motivated you?

Michael: The most inspiring moment is the cooperation with people from different traditions and from all over the globe. The diversity and the will to move together is what I find enriching and promising.

Risto: You have a rich experience, starting from a position as parish pastor. What have been your main fields of interest in the ecumenical life of the church?

Michael: The main fields in which I am engaged are mission studies and theological education. With mission I refer to the broad missio Dei *approach that ecumenical mission is about the church joining in God's mission and witnessing to God to the world in unity, interfaith dialogue, and joining in service, basically in the way that we explore in this book.*

Risto: This is a very broad perception of the ecumenical movement. It makes us participants in God's mission. Would you then affirm that working together is the focus of the ecumenical movement? Is this broad ecumenical movement only an action-oriented movement?

Michael: This definitely is a focus, particularly if we think about ecumenical networks and people associating to pursue common objectives. However, we should not overlook that the ecumenical movement and the mission movement are also spiritual movements.

Risto: I think that there you say something highly important. You recognize the importance of spirituality in the ecumenical movement. But is it not precisely spirituality that often separates us, when we do not know or understand how other Christians pray and worship God?

Michael: I believe that we witness not only in word and deed but also by the spirituality which guides us and empowers us. Missionary spirituality is one which transcends ecclesial and confessional boundaries.

UNITY AND FRAGMENTATION

IN 2022, CHURCH OF England Archbishop Justin Welby addressed the delegates of the World Council of Churches (WCC) assembly. In the plenary on "Christian Unity and the Churches' Common Witness" he spoke about a world in crisis and reminded the audience that "the luxurious expense of well-practiced Christian division is no longer affordable."[1] Visibly, it was a frustrated and critical comment on the situation of the ecumenical movement in general and the Anglican Communion in particular and he encouraged the plenary to be willing to take risks to step forward. His remark is here also taken as a critical comment on the cost of the energy, actions and reflection it takes to maintain fragmentation while coming together and staying together. Criticizing such costs is not a vote for giving up efforts of churches to come together. However, in the context of our overall topic of mission in times of many-sided crisis, it adds the crisis of fragmentation among the churches. In the ecumenical movement this seems to be mitigated by its well-practiced institutionalization.

This chapter will explore the tension between the urgent and important call for unity and the complacency of living with the existing divisions highlighted by Welby. It will be argued that mission in the Spirit can help to transcend the fragmentation in Christ's earthly body to move together. Coming to Christ, however, means joining a particular body of believers on earth. Ideas for a wider ecumenism will be proposed to at least reduce the tensions and to explore the extent to which mission is affected by the fragmentation. Can mission offer a viable solution to the mystery of the one church existing in many communities?

---

1. Welby in *Christ's Love Moves the World*, 303.

The Complacency We Need to Explode

PRACTICING CHRISTIAN DIVISION

Despite movements towards church unity, we are witnessing a fragmentation of the body of Christ and even new divisions in world Christianity. While we can perceive realignments such as overcoming the rift between evangelicals and ecumenicals in mission, even where there have been movements towards unity, we see new divisions and schisms. There have been splits in global church bodies such as the Methodist Church[2] and tensions for some years in the Anglican Communion.[3] We observe growing divisions in the Orthodox families, such as over the Ecumenical Patriarchate's granting autocephaly to the Orthodox Church of Ukraine in 2019. This move was strongly opposed by the Russian Orthodox Church, which regards Ukraine as its canonical territory. It eventually broke off relations with Constantinople over the issue. This also led to conflicts between those Orthodox churches that supported an autocephalous Orthodox Church of Ukraine and those who opposed it.[4] The WCC assembly at Karlsruhe was an example of attempts to mitigate the repercussions of war in the Ukraine[5] and of debate about Israel' settlements policy.[6] Power issues impacting the credibility of church unity are sobering when it comes to the churches' call for justice, peace, and reconciliation.

Welby's outcry is one of a person who holds an office which should be in itself a sign of unity through mutual recognition in the Anglican community—the seat of the Archbishop of Canterbury. We hear it is as an almost cynical comment which can be extended to other divisions. As Christians, we have become so used to our being divided and which we have learnt to practice so well that it no longer seems to hurt. A good example for this is the prayer tent at the WCC assembly at Karlsruhe in 2022. Being at the site, we learned that a building could not be completed in time and instead this tent was erected in the space between the different buildings in which the delegates came together. It served as the central place where the Bible studies and prayer times including singing took place. In many reports,

---

2. See the note on the launch of the split off Global Methodist Church, "Launch Information."

3. For the tensions in the Anglican Communion see the website of the Global Anglican Future Conference (GAFCON), critiquing any movement towards recognition of LGBTQI+. https://www.gafcon.org/about.

4. See Apostolou, "Official Recognition for Ukrainian Church Roils Orthodox World."

5. See *Christ's Love Moves the World*, 108–10.

6. See *Christ's Love Moves the World*, 202–6.

these times under the "heavenly" roof were praised as a time of celebrating and experiencing a shared spirituality in diversity, bringing together the richness and charisms of the different traditions, creating moving moments of praying together and listening to the word of God. The unplanned and transient structure seems to have given some flesh to the image of the pilgrimage of justice and peace evoked by the assembly—God's people on the move. However, it was a moment of living a well-practiced Christian division, because the tent is like a roof covering up a void. For ecclesiological and theological reasons, it is not possible to have a common worship service, Eucharist, or liturgy. Clarity and transparency in ecclesiological matters is to be appreciated—but the question arises how this unity in practicing spirituality experienced so joyfully by the participants relates to the unity that cannot be practiced according to the churches to which they belong. Does the fear that something *could* happen have greater force than any willingness to risk exploring deeper unity which could replace the expenses of practicing division so well and luxuriously—to the extent of even avoiding the word "service"?

The division in the understanding of ministry and Eucharist seems to be fundamental and insurmountable. Looking back into the history of the ecumenical movement, we can find glimpses of hope. Fifty years ago, no one would have imagined that the Roman Catholic Church and the Lutheran Churches would be able to recognize each other's doctrine of justification, which was the symbol—also in the dogmatic meaning of the word—of a conflict that had the power to tear apart the European continent five hundred years ago. Then, the *Joint Declaration on the Doctrine of Justification* was signed by the Pontifical Council for Promoting Christian Unity and the Lutheran World Federation in 1999.[7] The World Council of Methodist Churches joined the declaration in 2006 and the World Communion of Reformed Churches in 2017. The Anglican Communion also announced its agreement in 2017, meaning that the Joint Declaration is recognized by five major churches or church families.[8] In contrast to these rapprochements—to which we can add those on baptism—nothing seems to be possible when it comes to the question of the Eucharist.[9] In the context of the five hundredth jubilee of reformation, a joint service of the Roman Catholic Church and the Lutheran World Federation took place in

---

7. *Joint Declaration on the Doctrine of Justification.*

8. Anglican Communion, "Resolution 16.17."

9. Even though the churches acknowledge the process *Baptism, Eucharist and Ministry*.

The Complacency We Need to Explode

Lund, Sweden. Again, we observe a luxurious expense. The service took place 499 years after the Reformation and yet the church representatives coming together to commemorate and to celebrate Christ were not able to share the Eucharist.[10] The presence of female bishops at this service in Lund is an indication not only of the divide between the Roman Catholic Church and the Lutherans, but also of one of the painful points within the Lutheran World Federation, which has been struggling for decades over the ordination of women.[11]

In the context of the world's crises and the fragmentation of the body of Christ, it is remarkable that such an event was possible, and congratulations to those who were able to bring people together. However, the effort was also aimed at preventing certain issues from coming to the surface. The point emphasized here is, however, that from the perspective of churches participating in God's mission (*missio Dei*), the question is what such a carefully orchestrated event communicates—unity?

A painful observation is that while there is a growing consensus on doctrinal and ecclesiological issues that allows divisions to be overcome,[12] this does not seem possible for the growing divisions within world communions and churches on political and ethical issues. In our world in crisis there are enough pressing issues to discuss, such as wars, how to respond to the climate crisis, the use or misuse of power and corruption in the churches, racism, or growing nationalism in many churches. So why is it that homosexuality, same-sex relationships, and women's ordination are chosen for battle? Why are issues that are social-ethical issues—which means that according to a Protestant perspective we can live with some diversity on these issues—turned into confessional issues that make communion in reconciled diversity impossible and lead to divisions? In all of this the Bible seems to be used as an arsenal of weapons to fight over this issue, not as a common basis on which to reconcile diversity.

At the first WCC assembly in 1948 in Amsterdam, the delegates emphasized that their churches wanted to "stay together" after the destruction and violence before and during the Second World War. There had been some movements for peace among Christians during the First World War,

---

10. Joint Catholic-Lutheran Commemoration of The Reformation, "Joint Ecumenical Commemoration."

11. *Participation of Women in the Ordained Ministry.*

12. Beyond the mentioned agreements, see, for example, Gros, *Growth in Agreement II.*

nevertheless, the Christians in virtually all European countries presented themselves as people commissioned by God to liberate the world from God's enemies. Only to destroy the enemy would bring peace, justice, and world in safety.[13] This look into the past is a pointer to one of the reasons why the first WCC constitution from 1948 did not speak of unity but of "ecumenical consciousness" which was linked to mission. Two of the main "functions" of the Council were to "promote the growth of ecumenical consciousness in the members of all churches" and "to support the churches in their task of evangelism."[14] In 1961, at the first Assembly held outside the Western World, in New Delhi, the main function of the WCC was defined as "to carry on the work of the world movements for faith and order and life and work" as in 1948 to which now was added "and of the International Missionary Council" and "to support the churches in their worldwide missionary and evangelistic task."[15] In New Delhi, we find a section on unity in which we read, "Unity is not of our making, but as we receive the grace of Jesus Christ we are one in him. We are called to bear witness to the gift of unity through offering our lives as sacrifices to his glory. The fact that we are living in division shows that we have not realized God's gift of unity and we acknowledge our disobedience before him."[16]

The Unity Statement issued and accepted at the WCC assembly in Karlsruhe in 2022 looks back to the statements of the various assemblies.[17] The unity statement from the Busan assembly in 2013 emphasized the unity of the church as a sign pointing to the reconciling of all humankind and "of the whole of creation itself, the whole inhabited earth." At this assembly, the churches committed themselves to "moving together" on the pilgrimage of justice and peace and the pilgrimage was reconfirmed at the Karlsruhe assembly.[18]

Karlsruhe was a call to unity and united action in justice, peace—with then the focus on the war in Ukraine—and the climate crisis which was a priority. A learning experience both of the ecumenical and the mission movement is that these issues overlap and permeate each other, even though the climate crisis has overshadowed everything as a common challenge and

13. Greschat, *Der Erste Weltkrieg und die Christenheit*, 76.
14. Visser 't Hooft, *Man's Disorder and God's Design*, 197–98.
15. *New Delhi Report*, 426–43, at 427.
16. *New Delhi Report*, 116–35, at 118.
17. *Christ's Love Moves the World*, 10–19.
18. *Christ's Love Moves the World*, 14, 17.

threat to "life in fullness" (TTL). The documents of the World Mission Conference in Athens (2005)[19] and those of the International Convocation on Just Peace in Kingston, Jamaica (2011),[20] demonstrate this convergence of topics in the mission movement. It was also evident in the five thematic assembly plenaries held in Karlsruhe under the themes: Unity, Reconciliation, Wholeness of Life, Creation and Destruction, Common Witness, and Europe. The climate crisis, war and reconciliation, justice and peace, gender and empowerment played a role in all plenaries and many of the ecumenical conversations, as well as in the workshops offered in the fringe program.[21]

At the assembly, unity was maintained in face of massive conflicts. This is remarkable, and some opined that this could be the testimony of the churches to the world. It would be encouraging to see efforts focused not so much on painstakingly preserving division, but on using the lines of conflict as a vantage point from which to make progress. However, ecumenism is a slow and arduous process.

NAVIGATING ECUMENISM

Some history books display the history of the churches as a tree. The existing churches and movements are, so to speak, the tips of the branches, all coming from the same root. This illustrates well that the present situation of diversity of churches in the world is to a great extent the result of separation, fragmentation, and division in history. This simplistic picture has some truth, as in the case of the schism in the West between the Roman Catholic Church and the Reformation movements. It urges us to recognize that attempts at unity take place on the back of a history of conflict and fragmentation in the midst of current conflicts. However, the tree image is misleading when trying to place in this picture, for example, Pentecostal, Charismatic, or independent movements that draw on different streams of the Christian tradition. Perhaps a more appropriate image would be that of a rhizome, of plants which do not have individual roots but are interconnected beneath the surface.[22] In the perspective of this analogy the surface looks like a tapestry of many churches and Christian communities existing

19. Matthey, *"Come, Holy Spirit, Heal and Reconcile!"*
20. *Just Peace Companion.*
21. *Christ's Love Moves the World.*
22. For the concept of rhizome see Deleuze and Guattari, *Thousand Plateaus.*

side by side but under the surface they are interconnected in multiple ways. Although we can see a development in time, none of them can be identified as the sole origin. They remain connected, even after they split or separated from each other. This suggests that the attempt to identify the moments of splits is part of the hermeneutics on how churches trace their own history and dogmatics. A telling example is that in history books we find that the year 1054 is usually given for the schism between the Western (Pope) church and the Eastern Church (Patriarchate). But this is an afterthought. In 1054, only a relatively small number of individuals had excommunicated each other. It was necessary to develop the interpretation of this event up to the reciprocal excommunication of the whole body of churches and to embody this interpretation in the self-understanding of the churches—so that the schism grew over the decades into the full schism of the churches as it has been practiced ever since.[23]

With this example we argue that division could be considered as a crisis mitigated by practicing it. By practicing it, it is inscribed into the organisms by incorporating the reasons for being different into their identity and structure, as they evolve over time. Overcoming the conflict would, therefore, require a change in the identity embodied in practice which is much more difficult to attain than to reinterpret differences in beliefs. An example is the discussion about the mutual condemnations as heretics in the sixteenth century that led to the schisms in the Reformation movements. In dialogues in which these declarations were revisited in the twenty-first century, the representatives explained that the condemnations of their respective predecessors in the sixteenth century do not apply to the representatives of the churches today. This made it possible to maintain the confessions, such as the Augsburg Confession, and to continue to use the confessions by muting the condemnations in them. This allowed for acts of repentance and ecumenical relations, while the discussion on the concrete embodied practices of the different churches continued.[24]

MISSION AS A VANTAGE POINT

The problem with the tree metaphor for the multiplicity of churches mentioned above is that it insinuates a lineage as a history of separation. The rhizomatic metaphor can help to perceive more clearly that even with a

23. See more details on this argument in Biehl, "Zur Zukunft des Christentums."
24. See for example, *Bearing Fruit*.

somehow shared root—as it were underground, in the picture—today's mosaic of world Christianity is the result of churches which sprang up at different places and times, connected in many cases by rather thin lines of continuity. Such a metaphor helps to map particularly the cases in which the churches or communities could not easily be placed in the tree picture because their origin is not so easily traceable. The "plants" above the ground, to remain in the picture of the rhizome, are the result of embodied practices in church orders, constitutions, polity, and confessional status which override the common root by marking the churches through their developed consciousness of difference. Developing the metaphor of the rhizome to understand the tapestry of world Christianity leads to a different image that might allow us to take mission as the vantage point for a wider ecumenism. This, in turn, could reintroduce an idea of unity not in origin but in hope and in motion which is capable of overcoming the complacency of well-practiced divisions.

The critical debates in Europe on mission revolve around the embodied practice of mission in the nineteenth and early twentieth centuries, when mission took place in an imperial setting. Mission was the sending of emissaries, called missionaries, beyond the realm of the self-defined Christian world. Report I of the Edinburgh conference (1910) spoke of "carrying the gospel to the non-Christian world." The aim of mission, so understood, is to turn the latter into a copy of the former. To go beyond this spatial understanding of mission, the formula of mission from "everywhere to everywhere" was promoted at the 2010 Jubilee Conference at Edinburgh. This formula recognizes the existence of multiple centers. However, it still seems to have the flavor that mission is about moving and being sent.

Dana Robert takes the discussion forward by evoking the image of "a network, an international web of human relationships in which the 'missionaries' scamper back and forth like human spiders, weaving and expanding the web in all directions. It is important to study the spiders, but it is equally important to notice the web." She speaks of a "multi-cultural, global matrix" of mission.[25] The concept of a matrix—which comes close to the analogy of the rhizome—seems better suited to account for mission in our world today because it does not focus on movement alone. People are moving—but most of them stay, even in most desperate situations. This is confirmed by the statistics of the *Atlas of Global Christianity* that estimates that 70 percent of the growth of Christianity (1910–2020), predominantly

---

25. Robert, *Christian Mission*, 176.

in the Global South, is due to (Christian) population growth. Only about 24 percent is due to conversions, which could be counted as the result of missionary activity.[26]

The image of a matrix and the metaphor of the rhizome present a world that is not divided according to mission strategies to change the world at certain places. Both concepts present the globe as the space in which mission is happening, whether by staying at a particular place or moving to another one. This brings a shift in perspective. Mission *happens everywhere*, and some of it occurs because people move. A minority of people may be sent or feel called to move and evangelize, while the much larger part bear witness where they live. Those moving, move in a web of relationships that should be studied and uncovered, not just the missionaries moving in it. Such an approach broadens our understanding of mission.

There are well-defined and well-structured churches in mission, communicating the gospel in their context, not only in the Global North. They are the churches that form the ecumenical space with well-defined ecumenical relationships, dialogues about their confessional statuses among them and joining regional or global fellowships defined by a constitution. They may interpret their mission as proclaiming the gospel where they are, reaching out primarily to the people around them. Many of them are not so strong in sending cross-cultural missionaries, because in their logic in the other regions there is a church of the same family or fellowship or a partner church. These churches would be the agent of mission, so no need to send missionaries.

The mission matrix encompasses also organizations that understand their mission as sending people across borders into different cultures. They are not churches and may in principle disagree with the perception of the churches when it comes to why and where mission is necessary. The different logics and practices embodied in these two different entities may explain why it is difficult to define their relationship in the mission documents of the ecumenical world. Gerrit Noort, then from the Mission Council in the Netherlands, questioned TTL: "Why is there no reference to missionaries in a total of 112 articles, with the possible exception of article 76, which refers to mission trips."[27]

---

26. Johnson and Ross, *Atlas of Global Christianity*, 64.

27. Noort, "'So What?,'" 195. TTL seems to be critical of the short-term trips, see Keum, *Together Towards Life*, §76.

We read TTL as prioritizing mission in the Spirit and evangelism, with the local congregations as the main agent in mission. TTL speaks about para-church missionary organizations in two paragraphs, without really defining the relationship between them and the churches.

"While discussions of unity have been very concerned with structural questions, mission agencies can represent flexibility and subsidiarity in mission. While para-church movements can find accountability and direction through ecclesial mooring, para-church structures can help churches not to forget their dynamic apostolic character" (TTL, §64, see §63).

We find the opposite in the Lausanne movement which is a mission minded movement. The Cape Town document (2010) is about doing and organizing mission and evangelism by Christian leaders. "Its goal? To bring a fresh challenge to the global church to bear witness to Jesus Christ and all his teaching—in every nation, in every sphere of society, and in the realm of ideas."[28] In turn, it talks about the global church, the description of which remains vague and without contours.

All of these and many more different understandings of mission are part of the global mission matrix. We should use the different emphases of mission for a discerning process through reciprocal criticisms of practices and theologies. Such a debate may show that some of them are not conducive in a given context, lead to conflict or do not reflect authentic evangelism. The quoted study on the number of worldwide missionaries reveals, for example, that surprisingly the majority of the cross-cultural missionaries are sent to countries in which we find also a majority of Christians.[29] This can be read as a critique of the mission of local and probably well-structured churches. Can it be valid to define mission by discerning mission fields and target groups without taking into account the existence of churches in the area?

IN WAY OF A CONCLUSION

If we step outside the confines of the well-structured ecumenical world into the realities and diversity of world Christianity, mission can be freed from being an organized and strategic activity and transformed into the art of discerning the presence of God in the Spirit everywhere. Following such an approach, Michael Biehl wrote in a paper on prophetic mission: "Mission

28. *Cape Town Commitment*, 7.
29. *Christianity in Its Global Context*, 77.

[in the Western world] is not so much necessary because people are not or no longer Christians. Mission is necessary to bear witness to God's invitation and hospitality. Evangelism is the attempt to live out this gift in such an inviting way that others can see what we stand for, where we stand and what motivates us."[30]

Stephen Bevans links transforming discipleship and mission in the Spirit in his reflection on transforming discipleship, which he understands a the discerning the Spirit from the spirits, singling out the traces of God's presence in the situation in which people live together. Communicating the gospel then means facing together the challenge of the Spirit to make God's justice and mercy present, and to make mercy emerge and work.[31]

Such an understanding transforms mission so that it becomes prophetic and calls churches to become(!) communities of justice and peace which can be linked to the ecumenical pilgrimage of justice and peace. Prophetic mission means "discernment" in this communion of journeying, that is, discerning where and through whom God's Spirit is still at work. In Matt 25:31–46, Jesus Christ, as the Judge of the world, judges people on whether they have done works of love without asking for a reward or profit. Those who are judged ask in amazement when what they have done for others has benefited Christ? When did they ever meet him? The Judge of the world answers, whatever you did for one of the least of these sisters or brothers of mine, you did for me. These are the works that today are mainly attributed to the diaconate: visiting prisoners and the sick, feeding or clothing the poor (cf. the above quotation from Isaiah in Luke 4). But these works can also be understood as a sign of resistance to the conditions that force people to live in such conditions. This is the political dimension of diaconia and advocacy.[32]

The passage on judgment opens up the possibility of interpreting people's actions prophetically in terms of the love of Christ, also of those who do not share the faith in him. This becomes possible when mission is not only determined by the actions of those who consciously follow Christ. *Missio Dei* is broader than, and not limited to, the actions of churches or individual Christians. It is the Holy Spirit who empowers people as "missionaries" to live out God's love, mercy, and justice in this world. Through the Spirit, the actions and faith of people who do not confess this God can

---

30. Biehl, "Prophetische Mission," 437 (our translation).
31. Bevans, "Together Towards Life," 156–57.
32. See Dowsett, *Evangelisation and Diaconia in Context*.

be evaluated in the light of the gospel—without appropriating their deeds or forcing them to become members of Christian congregations.

In this way, prophetic mission invites us to the adventure of walking together into a future that is believed to be changeable. It encourages, especially when not all share the same faith, the promotion of values and attitudes as a sign of mission in encounter and communion, which do not allow mercy to fade, and which work for justice, reconciliation, and peace. This communion on the way can include all those who share the values and objectives mentioned above, even if they do not share the Christian reason and motivation. In the communion of walking with the many in society, the witness of our faith becomes one of respect for the faith of others. The point of transformation here would be openness to the activity of God, who not only blesses lived engagement, but includes it in God's eschatological promise. As Christians, we are always on the way: The consummation is yet to come, but the Spirit is already transforming here and now what we experience and live, what we hope and believe. This leads to mission in hope (see ch. 11).

If we work thus from the matrix of relationships including people on the move, mission could become the disturbance of the complacency of the luxurious expense of Christian division because it liquefies the expression of the Christian faith by living it in contextual realities of today, beyond structures and ecumenical agreements. One of the consequences of this idea could be to think more about the ways in which many movements in the world are influenced by religious people and therefore by those with a "mission orientation," even though from various backgrounds. But we also need to acknowledge that they in turn are influenced by movements, moods, changing attitudes, and new perspectives. At the WCC assembly in Karlsruhe there was a strong impetus for acknowledging the existence, identities, and rights of a diversity of movements. Strong voices were heard challenging the churches for inclusion of people with disabilities, indigenous peoples, LGBTQi+, migrants, marginalized groups. . . .This means that the diversity of the world enters the church and mission transforms them from within. Accepting and acknowledging the inner diversity may help its capacity to transcend divisions in moving together without investing so much in the luxurious expense of well-practiced difference.

10

The Triune God We Need to Adore in Unity

Marina: Risto, you have worked as Mission Director both on a global ecumenical level (World Council of Churches' Commission on World Mission and Evangelism) and a national church level (Evangelical Lutheran Church of Finland). Why do you so strongly emphasize the interconnectedness of mission and unity?

Risto: My experience is that it cannot be otherwise. Mission cannot be anything else but ecumenical, in the full sense of the word, because Christians cannot give their witness to Christ separately and be credible at the same time. The triune God is one, and each Christian has his or her personal story, but their faith is the same in the same God. I have seen how the love of Christ unites people of various Christian denominations and churches in mission. They are one so that the world may believe. Unity without mission is reduced or truncated unity, and mission without unity is not credible in the eyes of those who are not Christians. We need to keep these two, mission and unity, together.

Marina: We know that not all Christians are ready to work together. What would you say to them?

Risto: I have seen that Christians of various backgrounds can come together and do mission work together. They do not necessarily agree on everything, but one thing is sure: Christians are called to love one another. This love is given by the missionary God who has first loved human beings

(John 3:16; 1 John 4:19). And yet, this love does not stop with Christians who experience the love of God in Christ and in the power of the Spirit. The divine love is there for everybody. This is God's mission.

Marina: *Why do you consider convergence between the ecumenical and evangelical mission movements so important?*

Risto: *"Ecumenical" and "evangelical" are words used often unfortunately only as labels to underline boundaries, limits, and differences. God is much more, beyond our imagination. If the missionary God, who calls us and sends us all to mission, cannot be put in a box, why should we try to do that to other Christians and give them labels? We can simply read the Acts of Apostles. There are differences and difficulties among the followers of Christ but not about the one being "ecumenical" and the other "evangelical." They were all Christians (Acts 11:26).*

UNITY, BOTH THEOLOGICALLY AND historically, is based on the one and triune God and strongly connected with hope: "There is one body and one Spirit, just as you were called to the one hope of your calling" (Eph 4:4). There is hope for a better world and for the future. This hope should encourage Christians to show to the world in crisis that they are one and love each other.

Hope in unity implies that there should be no division between the church's unity and its mission as seems to be the case, in particular, and notoriously, in Protestant Christianity. "Mission people" and "unity people" are often two separate groups, organizationally and theologically. Even in the structures of Protestant Christianity in the twentieth century we have had the International Missionary Council (IMC, established 1921) and the World Council of Churches (WCC, established 1948). Since the two global ecumenical organizations later merged at the Assembly of the WCC in New Delhi in 1961, there have been two separate structures within one organization, the WCC Commission on Faith and Order and the WCC Commission on World Mission and Evangelism (CWME). The separation of mission and unity continues today, conceptually and structurally.

Further, there is another serious division even within the Protestant mission movement which is related to the one mentioned above. Following the New Delhi Assembly in 1961 and the first CWME conference on World Mission and Evangelism in Mexico City in 1963, almost one thousand evangelical missionaries and mission leaders attended a Congress on the Church's Worldwide Mission in Wheaton, Illinois, in 1966. Later the same year, 1,100 delegates gathered in Berlin for an evangelical "World Congress of Evangelism."[1] A Roman Catholic observer in Berlin noted that the latter "generated new confidence among Evangelicals and new taste for battle with those who slight, if not disdain or disown, direct evangelism."[2] After the WCC Assembly in Uppsala in 1968 these evangelical Christians became even more distanced from the WCC and the CWME, and they organized the International Congress on World Evangelism in Lausanne in 1974, giving birth to the Lausanne Committee for World Evangelization and its global meetings.

However, both divisions are—and have always been—theologically unsound and practically injurious.[3] Even if the two concepts of unity and mission are not identical, they both are insufficient in themselves, that is, mission without unity is divisive to the church, and unity without mission is like an empty shell, lacking a dynamic and loving character of God's mission. "If there is one thing which the history of the modern missionary movement has taught us, it is that you cannot engage in world mission without being compelled to face questions of unity."[4] The division within the Protestant mission movement in the second half of the twentieth century is recent and unnecessary, because every follower of Jesus, who takes Jesus's life, death, and resurrection seriously, is both "ecumenical" and "evangelical," in the deepest sense of both words. It can be observed that there have been deep commitments to world mission and evangelism on both sides, "ecumenicals" and "evangelicals," and that both sides have failed to give the other enough space and voice, listening and encountering, which has led to false images of the other—created most of the time at a distance, not in dialogue with the other. And yet, as with the discussion on "mission and unity," both have the same point of departure, the same origin: the triune God and the task of Jesus Christ given to his followers. The theological reason for the oneness of "ecumenicals" and "evangelicals" is that these movements are based in the oneness of the triune God and the triune God's missionary nature. The Trinity is the mystery of salvation, a central Christian doctrine, and the guarantee of the oneness of Christians and churches. Without it, the Jesus movement would have been very different.

1. Thomas, *Missions and Unity*, 139–40.
2. Stransky, "World Congress," 15.
3. Some important consequences of divisions are presented by Kim, "Mission: Integrated or Autonomous?," 62–80.
4. Newbigin, *One Body One Gospel One World*, 53–54.

We will first deal with unity and mission in the Trinity, and then the issue of "ecumenical" vs. "evangelical."

UNITY AND MISSION IN THE TRINITY

The starting point of the Christian doctrine of the Trinity can be traced back to the experiences of the first disciples of Jesus. For them, he was more than a human being, he prayed to his Father, and he spoke about Father and the Spirit. After the experience of the first Pentecost the first followers of Jesus gradually gained an understanding of God who was One in Three, and Three in One. A purely unitarian or monolithic idea of God would not have been adequate to express their dynamic and personal experience of God. In the New Testament texts, the idea of divinity being "Father, Son, and Spirit" can be found literally mentioned in Matt 28:19 and 2 Cor 13:14. But there are several other passages indicating the Oneness in Trinity (e.g. 1 Cor 12:4–6; Gal 4:6; Titus 3:4–6).

During the first centuries, not without ecclesial and civil power struggles, the doctrine of the Trinity was debated. Especially important milestones have been the Council of Nicaea in 325, which was the first ecumenical council, and the Second Ecumenical Council of Constantinople in 381. It was believed that "at stake was indeed something belonging to the *status confessionis* and not a matter of indifference (*adiaphora*), a metaphysical issue, or a mere question of semantics."[5]

For various reasons, at the beginning of the twentieth century the doctrine of the Trinity was in the background when Christian theology was discussed. In the course of the twentieth century, two famous theologians, the reformed Karl Barth (1886–1968) and the Catholic Karl Rahner (1904–84), are often named as the main architects behind a strong renewal of a theological interest in the doctrine of the Trinity, especially in the latter half of the century. "It took a Barth and a Rahner to make the Trinity not only the central doctrine of the Christian faith but also the structural principle of Christian theology."[6]

---

5. Phan, "Developments of the Doctrine of the Trinity," 11. We cannot go here into a detailed chronological and substantial development of the doctrine of the Trinity in the history of Christian theology.

6. Phan, "Developments of the Doctrine of the Trinity," 11. Another reason for the increased interest in the Trinity was undoubtedly the birth of the modern Pentecostal movement in 1906 (Azusa Street revival in Los Angeles) and its emphasis on the Spirit, as well as the "discovery" of the theology and liturgy of the Eastern tradition by the

Barth has famously affirmed that "the doctrine of the Trinity is what basically distinguishes the Christian doctrine of God as Christian, and therefore what already distinguishes the Christian concept of revelation as Christian, in contrast to all other possible doctrines of God or concepts of revelation."[7] For him, there must be a correspondence between the revealing God (the Father) and the self-revelation of God (the Son). Barth argues that a recognition of revelation as divine self-revelation cannot be achieved by sinful humanity, so it must be the work of God—God the Spirit.

Rahner is likewise famous for his basic thesis that "the 'economic' Trinity is the 'immanent' Trinity and the 'immanent' Trinity is the 'economic' Trinity."[8] "Immanent" means transcendental, eternal mutual relationships in God, whereas "economic" means the three persons' actions on behalf of human beings. In other words, God known in God's actions corresponds to how God actually is. The three persons are the one and the same God. And the human experience of God's actions is a real experience of God's inner life.

Within a longer historical perspective, the two theologians only went back to the very roots of the Christian doctrine. As indicated above, there is no full-fledged doctrine of the Trinity available in the New Testament. Christians are firmly monotheists (see, e.g., Deut 6:4; Eph 4:5–6), but in a different way than Jews or Muslims. Christians believe in the God who is One-in-Three and Three-in-One. The Father is God, the Son Jesus is God, the Spirit is God.[9] Recognizing this *koinonia* theologically and in the life of the church opens doors to a better understanding of the character and role of the church in this world, and through them, challenges that Christians—as followers of Christ, but always with other human beings—are facing today.

Barth, Rahner, and other Western theologians are not far from the understanding of the Eastern Christianity of the Trinity, in which creation by God the Father, redemption in Jesus the Son, and salvation within and without the church in the power of the Holy Spirit are understood in the frame of the inner life of the Trinity, in the context of mutual communion

---

ecumenical movement, with its trinitarian pneumatology.

7. Barth, *Church Dogmatics*, 1/1:301. He also remarks that "in putting the doctrine of the Trinity at the head of all dogmatics we are adopting a very isolated position from the standpoint of dogmatic history," 300.

8. Rahner, *Trinity*, 22.

9. See, for example, Jukko, "Doctrine of the Trinity."

and love between the three persons. The implications for mission of the Orthodox theology are important.[10]

As the roles of the three persons of the Trinity are different, there is the Father sending the Son, and the Father, through the Son (or the Western addition: "and the Son"—the famous *filioque*),[11] sending the Spirit. The Latin word to describe this event is *missio*, derived from the verb *mittere*, to send. Sending, *missio*, has become a standard word to describe the saving act of God in the world. And God uses people to carry out divine plans for the world. The first disciples were often fragile. Even at the encounter of the risen Jesus, "some doubted" (Matt 28:17). And when Jesus appeared to his disciples and Thomas was not there, he did not believe the word of the others (John 20:25). And yet, Jesus commissioned them to go and make disciples (Matt 28:19–20), and he breathed on them and asked them to receive the Holy Spirit (John 20:22).

Especially recent ecumenical missiology has picked up both the term and idea of the triune and missionary God. The triune God is a missionary God, and God starts mission in Godself (Father-Son-Spirit), and continues this action in, and for, the world. This means that God and God's salvific action have been there before there was any church or any missionary activity. Mission is an attribute of God. The missionary God is working in the world, and this act is called *missio Dei*. The role of human beings is to participate in *missio Dei*, God's mission.

This term, *missio Dei*, was theologically developed at the International Missionary Council meeting in Willingen in 1952 even if not specifically mentioned *ipsissima verba* at the meeting. It was launched by Karl Hartenstein,[12] the mission director of the Basel Mission, and has been used extensively since then in missiology. However, it was—not surprisingly—Karl Barth who was one of the first theologians to describe mission as God's mission, the missionary God's own activity.[13] The concept took mission into the Trinity—and to mission theology. This shift has meant a radical move in missiological thinking from soteriology and ecclesiology right into

---

10. See, e.g., Vassiliadis, *Orthodox Perspectives*; Istavridis, "Orthodox Churches," 297–98.

11. On *filioque*, see, e.g., Hilberat, "Filioque II. Systematisch-theologisch."

12. In particular in 1933 by Hartenstein, *Die Mission als theologisches Problem*.

13. Barth gave a presentation at the Brandenburg Missionary Conference in Berlin in 1932. His paper, "Die Theologie und die Mission in der Gegenwart," can be found in Karl Barth, *Theologische Fragen und Antworten*, 100–126.

the "middle" of the triune God. It is the triune God sending the church into the world. The church exists because there is mission.

However, after the Willingen meeting in 1952 the ecumenical scope of the understanding of the term has widened to display how God's mission affects all people and takes place in human history, not only in and through the church. In fact, radicalized views suggested that *missio Dei* even excluded the church's involvement and that the church had become unnecessary for God's mission. The world would have no need for the missionary contribution of Christians: "God is not imaginable without the reconciled world, neither the world without God's dynamic presence."[14] *Missio Dei* has been described as a "Trojan horse through which the (unassimilated) 'American' vision was fetched into the well-guarded walls of the ecumenical theology of mission."[15] Even if the use of *missio Dei* has been challenged, it has undoubtedly shifted the focus of mission to the triune God, without whom there would be no mission. "Mission has its origin in the heart of God. God is a fountain of sending love. This is the deepest source of mission. It is impossible to penetrate deeper still; there is mission because God loves people."[16] Though there might be very different understandings of *missio Dei*, there is no return to a narrower concept of mission.

The change of the title of the 1912-founded ecumenical missiological journal, the *International Review of Missions*, to *International Review of Mission*, is a pertinent example of a change in the theological and practical understanding of mission and unity due to a trinitarian understanding of mission. When previously "missions"—in plural form—had been understood to mean particular organized attempts within the worldwide mission movement, mainly from the West to the rest of the world, at bringing the gospel to places where there was no presence of the gospel, or its presence was weak, now the meaning of "mission" was widened to denote God's actions in the world and Jesus as the ultimate example and his promise as the motivation of those actions: "As the Father has sent me, so I send you" (John 20:21). This promise was given to the first church, his closest disciples. Mission, it was understood, was carried out by the one, holy, catholic,

---

14. Bosch, *Transforming Mission*, 391–92.

15. Rosin, *Missio Dei*, 26. Cited in Bosch, *Transforming Mission*, 392.

16. Bosch, *Transforming Mission*, 392. Compare with the WCC mission affirmation *Together Towards Life: Mission and Evangelism in Changing Landscapes* (§2; §19): "Mission begins in the heart of the Triune God and the love that binds together the Holy Trinity overflows to all humanity and creation. . . . Mission is the overflow of the infinite love of the Triune God."

and apostolic church[17] through its members, starting with the first disciples of Jesus, wherever they have been, up until to our generation in the 2020s. However, the dropping of just one letter (an "s" of the plural) in the title of a missiological journal may not be easily followed by Christians all over the world: "If the business of mission is every Christian's business . . . there is the danger that no one will make it his [sic] business to go to the two billion who still have not heard, or who have given no response at all either of acceptance or rejection to the Gospel."[18]

ECUMENICAL AND EVANGELICAL

The 1960s was a turbulent period in world history with student riots in Paris and elsewhere in 1968, the invasion of Czechoslovakia in 1968, the Vietnam War, the Cultural Revolution in China, and the confrontation between fascism and communism in Latin America, among other things. This polarization of attitudes on all levels of society was also happening within Western Christianity, and critical voices could be heard on both sides.

Differences and radical critique, even polarization in the theological understanding both in the USA and Europe, did not leave intact either mission or evangelism. Even if at the very last meeting of the International Missionary Council in Delhi in November 1961 the plan of integration was adopted with only two member Councils deciding to withdraw from membership (the Congo Protestant Council and the Norwegian Missionary Council), there was still an uneasiness with the idea of the WCC itself and the fear of mission being swallowed and submerged into the structures of the WCC, weakening the missionary concern of the church. It was especially present in the USA, where some mission organizations opposed very strongly any association with the WCC. As already mentioned, in Berlin in 1966 some 1,100 delegates gathered for an ad hoc world congress of evangelism, with Billy Graham as the honorary chairman. The majority of the participants represented those "evangelicals" who were not satisfied with the merger of the IMC and the WCC, participants in the latter being considered "ecumenicals." The Berlin delegates wanted to clarify what

---

17. ". . . unam sanctam catholicam et apostolicam Ecclesiam." The so-called four marks of the church as expressed in the Niceno-Constantinopolitan Creed. See, e.g., Denzinger, *Kompendium*, 85.

18. Crane, "Editorial," 142.

is biblical evangelism.[19] In addition, the Berlin congress claimed to be the true successor of the Edinburgh 1910 World Missionary Conference.[20]

The word "evangelical" has a long history. It starts from the Greek word "εὐαγγέλιον," "good news," the gospel in the New Testament, through the time of Reformation in the sixteenth century (*evangelisch*) coming to the nineteenth century and the Evangelical Awakening on both sides of the Atlantic and the foundation of the Evangelical Alliance in 1846 and the American Branch of the Alliance in 1867. The Greek word is the root for "evangelicalism" that cannot be identified with any single Christian denomination, but whose main characteristics can be identified. They are the following four special marks of evangelical religion, in other words, priorities of evangelicalism: "*conversionism*, the belief that lives need to be changed; *activism*, the expression of the gospel in effort; *biblicism*, a particular regard for the Bible; and what may be called *crucicentrism*, a stress on the sacrifice of Christ on the cross."[21]

In the 1950s, Willem Adolf Visser 't Hooft, the first general secretary of the WCC, famously distinguished seven meanings of the word "oikoumenē," "ecumenical":

"(a) pertaining to or representing the whole (inhabited) earth; (b) pertaining to or representing the whole of the (Roman) Empire; (c) pertaining to or representing the whole of the Church; (d) that which has universal ecclesiastical validity; (e) pertaining to the world-wide missionary outreach of the Church; (f) pertaining to the relations between and unity of two or more Churches (or of Christians of various confessions); (g) that quality or attitude which expresses the consciousness of and desire for Christian unity."[22]

As can be seen in these meanings, all Christians, no matter what kind of religious conviction or theological understanding they may have, can use the word "ecumenical" of themselves. All Christians are "ecumenical." Its firm relatedness to mission can be seen, for example, in the name of a mission conference held in 1900 in New York: it "was called, significantly, the Ecumenical Missionary Conference 'because the plan of campaign which it proposes covers the whole area of the inhabited world.'"[23]

---

19. Stransky, "World Congress," 15.
20. Thomas, *Missions and Unity*, 140.
21. Bebbington, *Evangelicalism*, 2–3 (italics in the original).
22. Visser 't Hooft, "Word," 735.
23. Latourette, "Ecumenical Bearings," 354.

The decade between the congress of the "evangelicals" in Berlin in 1966 and the Assembly of the WCC ("ecumenicals") in Nairobi in 1975 was especially turbulent on the level of attitudes. Suspicions towards the newly established CWME in the structures of the WCC were increasing after the WCC Assembly in Uppsala 1968.[24] A sharp critique was addressed to the CWME/WCC in the area of world mission and, in particular, of evangelism. The main accusation by the evangelicals was that the CWME/WCC had "progressively watered down, even abandoned, the prime commitment to evangelism understood as the proclamation of the gospel of Christ in favour of a social, at worst revolutionary, approach to 'salvation' seen as worldly 'progress.'"[25]

However, especially with strong evangelical voices from Latin America such as René Padilla, Samuel Escobar, and Emilio Castro, the last mentioned speaking for the WCC, a total division of the global mission movement did not take place. Continuing to evaluate negatively the CWME/WCC, evangelicals gathered in 1974 in Lausanne for the International Congress on World Evangelization, or the First Lausanne Congress on World Evangelization (Lausanne I).[26] It seems, though, that in Lausanne 1974 "it was commonly admitted by the Evangelicals that the shape of their religion is influenced by the environment,"[27] in other words, that they were not independent of their social environment. Taking seriously the commitment to social dimension, John Stott was the main drafter of the so-called Lausanne Covenant, signed by almost all at the congress.[28] It soon became a kind of basis for the evangelical conception of mission and evangelism.

After the WCC Assembly in Nairobi in 1975, the heavy critique of the CWME/WCC especially from American evangelicals continued, but with reconciling efforts on both sides highly critical voices became few. On both sides there were influential leaders who spoke in favor of dialogue and respect for the other side, for example, Lesslie Newbigin, David J. Bosch, Mortimer Arias, as well as the already mentioned John Stott and Emilio Castro. One sign of this converging and reconciling movement is that numerous evangelical authors can be found as writers of the *International*

---

24. See, e.g., Winter, "Will Uppsala Betray the Two Billion?"
25. Conway, "Under Public Scrutiny," 440–41.
26. See Douglas, *Let the Earth Hear His Voice*.
27. Bebbington, *Evangelicalism*, 272.
28. Bebbington, *Evangelicalism*, 266. *The Lausanne Covenant* can be found, e.g., in Cameron, *Lausanne Legacy*, 3–53.

Review of Mission, the missiological journal of the IMC from 1921 and then of the WCC from 1961.

The evangelical mission movement that gathered in Lausanne in 1974 continued after the congress as the Lausanne Committee for World Evangelization, and is nowadays known as the Lausanne Movement.[29] There have been tensions between the Lausanne Movement and the CWME/WCC, and still in 1989 the Lausanne Movement organized its gathering in Manila in the same year as the CWME had its conference on world mission and evangelism in San Antonio, USA. The outcome of the Manila congress (the Second Lausanne Congress on World Evangelization, or Lausanne II) was the *Manila Manifesto*, which is a kind of elaboration of the Lausanne Covenant. The third Lausanne global congress was held in Cape Town in 2010 (the Third Lausanne Congress on World Evangelization, or Lausanne III), and its outcome document, the *Cape Town Commitment*, is a confession of faith written in a poetical "love language." It is also a call for action.[30] The fourth Lausanne Congress on World Evangelization (Lausanne IV) was held in Seoul, South Korea, in September 2024.[31]

UNITY AND ECUMENICAL AND EVANGELICAL MISSION

In 1982 Lesslie Newbigin, long-time missionary and bishop in India and the first director of the Commission on World Mission and Evangelism of the WCC, wrote that "all seriously committed Christians presumably believe that the gospel is for the whole world." He then binds together the two words, dealt with in this text, "evangel" and "oikoumenē" in a neat way: "The *evangel* is for the *oikoumenē*." Newbigin describes himself both as "evangelical" and "ecumenical."[32] This position is theologically well founded as explained above. When mission and church are both issued by one God who is a triune and missionary God, there is no reason to argue whether mission or unity should come first, as they both come first, as long as they both originate from, and contribute to, the great mission movement of God in the world. The universal church is missionary, but it needs "missions," i.e., mission organizations, networks, movements, groups, fellowships.

29. Lausanne Movement: https://lausanne.org/.
30. All three Lausanne documents are published in Cameron, *Lausanne Legacy*.
31. See Lausanne Movement, "Seoul Statement."
32. Newbigin, "Cross-Currents," 146.

There is still, however, the same relevant question that Newbigin asked a few decades ago: "Missionary societies and other specialized agencies have begun to provide in our day something of what these mobile ministries [apostles, prophets, and evangelists] provided for the early church, but they have never been integrated theoretically into our ecclesiologies or practically into our church orders. Is not this a real need of our time?"[33] Theology is still struggling with this question on the ecclesiological level.

If we take another level, that of global organizations, we can answer at least partly to Newbigin's inquiry. Historically and theologically, the WCC Commission on World Mission and Evangelism, the Lausanne Movement and the Mission Commission of the World Evangelical Alliance were originally one. The late Andrew Walls once remarked that both the "ecumenicals" and the "evangelicals" can trace their roots back to the Edinburgh World Missionary Conference 1910. "If each will go back to the pit whence both were dug, each may understand both themselves and the other better."[34] When the World Missionary Conference was staged in Edinburgh in 1910, there was no Mission Commission of the World Evangelical Alliance nor any Commission on World Mission and Evangelism of the WCC nor any Lausanne Committee for World Evangelization. The participants in Edinburgh in 1910 included various movements within world mission and various church bodies, and there was no division between the ecumenical and the evangelical Christians. Later, when the International Missionary Council was founded in 1921, as a natural continuation of the willingness to witness to Christ together in the world, the participants at the founding meeting at Lake Mohonk, USA, were representatives of the various Christian movements, "ecumenical" and "evangelical." Yet all agreed about the importance of a single common structure and also about the importance of recognizing that they all had a single task in common. In brief, this was the commission to proclaim the gospel the credibility of which was to be demonstrated by the unity of Christians, for which Jesus prayed (John 17:21).

Soon after the foundation of the WCC in 1948, the IMC found itself in a transitional situation because the churches founded by Western missionaries were growing and strengthening in their own mission tasks, and the relations between them, the national mission councils, and the WCC, and the role of the mission agencies and the ownership of mission were not clear and were in a state of flux and getting more complicated towards

33. Newbigin, "Cross-Currents," 150.
34. Walls, *Cross-Cultural Process*, 62.

the end of the colonial era. Towards the end of the 1950s it became clear that the church could not be a church if it was not a missionary church.[35] Thus the voices speaking for integration between the WCC and the IMC, proposing that the IMC should become part of the WCC, grew louder. In 1958 the International Missionary Council decided by an overwhelming majority to be integrated into the WCC, and this happened in 1961 in New Delhi, at the WCC's third assembly.

Since the 1960s, as explained above, history has seen a growing rift between so-called evangelicals, who thought that the WCC was concentrating too much on earthly matters, and so-called ecumenicals, who thought that the others were concentrating too much on a spiritual, "saving-your-soul" type of Christianity. Both descriptions are something of a caricature, but it has to be admitted that the WCC assembly in Uppsala in 1968 did place a heavy emphasis on societal, political, and ethical topics whereas evangelism was pushed aside. This in turn meant that the rift between the two movements was inexorably becoming an abyss, since the WCC position offered an understanding of mission as the action of God in society at large. The evangelical critics accused the WCC of being too much engaged in the social and political realm and of lacking a sufficiently clear theology of salvation. However, towards the end of the last century and in particular the first two decades of the twenty-first century there has been a slow but clear movement of convergence between the ecumenical and evangelical mission movements.

In 1982 the WCC published its first official mission statement entitled "Mission and Evangelism: An Ecumenical Affirmation."[36] This document was a deliberate attempt to build bridges between the ecumenicals and the evangelicals. Kenneth R. Ross in his function as a CWME advisor says: "It was a conciliatory document designed to encompass the characteristic concerns of each side in what had been a highly divisive debate."[37] The document attempts to bind together both personal conversion and decision to follow Christ, and prophetic social witness. Dogmatically speaking, this has been done with a strong Christological emphasis contained within a trinitarian framework.[38]

35. Cf. *Together Towards Life* (§58): "Thus the churches mainly and foremost need to be missionary churches."

36. "Mission and Evangelism: An Ecumenical Affirmation."

37. Ross, "Arusha Call," 446.

38. On relations between prophetic witness and missionary discipleship, see Jukko, "Toward Prophetic Missionary Discipleship."

For its part, the second mission affirmation adopted by the WCC was entitled *Together Towards Life: Mission and Evangelism in Changing Landscapes* (TTL). It was finalized and adopted in 2012 and presented to the member churches of the WCC in 2013 at the assembly in Busan, South Korea. It looks at spirituality, the margins, the church, and evangelism through a largely pneumatological lens. The statement contains four chapters, the titles of which are the following: 1) Spirit of Mission: Breath of Life; 2) Spirit of Liberation: Mission from the Margins; 3) Spirit of Community: Church on the Move; 4) Spirit of Pentecost: Good News for All (§11). What is most remarkable is that the section on evangelism, paragraphs 80–100 of the document, the hottest point of dispute between ecumenicals and evangelicals over forty years, was drafted jointly by the CWME and the Theological Commission of the World Evangelical Alliance. This can be seen as a strong sign of convergence or at least a sign of good theological cooperation, following the spirit in which the International Missionary Council was founded in 1921.

Another WCC mission document will be the third example of the movement of convergence between ecumenicals and evangelicals. This is the "Arusha Call to Discipleship," a major outcome of the WCC Arusha Conference on World Mission and Evangelism in 2018, which was adopted unanimously by the conference participants.[39] It is a short but powerful statement whose main emphasis is on transforming discipleship, in tune with *The Cape Town Commitment* (2010) with its notes of radical, obedient discipleship.[40] The "Arusha Call to Discipleship" urges us to remember that "the Holy Spirit continues to move us at this time and urgently calls us as Christian communities to respond with personal and communal conversion, and a transforming discipleship."[41] One of the fundamental ideas underlying the formulations of this CWME/WCC document is the notion that—as the "Arusha Conference Report" states—"it is not shared ideals that unite us, but rather our connectedness to Christ, our living Saviour and Lord."[42] This is the very same idea as expressed in *The Cape Town Commit-*

---

39. The document can be found in Jukko and Keum, *Moving in the Spirit*, 2–4.

40. Cameron, *Lausanne Legacy*, 160. "Disciple," "discipleship," and "disciple-making" also on pp. 106, 112, 120, 125 (in particular in connection with mission), 129, 142, 147–48, 155, 161. Discipleship can be found as a current theme in most Christian churches, starting with Pope Francis's emphasis on missionary disciples (*Evangelii Gaudium*, §120).

41. Jukko and Keum, *Moving in the Spirit*, 2.

42. Jukko and Keum, *Moving in the Spirit*, 10. "Arusha Conference Report."

ment when it speaks about "Christ-centred leaders."[43] At the same time, the "Arusha Call to Discipleship" also expresses concerns about social issues and contemporary crises. Thus, the mission document deliberately builds bridges of convergence and unity between ecumenicals and evangelicals. The document is based on the importance of meeting with the other, of listening to one another and considering one another's concerns, and also, ultimately, of using language that makes sense to everyone.

RECONCILED IN UNITY

Through the centuries, in various struggles, Christians have shown great resilience and they have boldly moved in mission and evangelism. Even if it has been theologically understood that God is simultaneously one and triune—and missionary—and that there is a divine missionary movement of love that sends, at the practical level Christians have often been divided by negligible, non-theological reasons, and this splitting is still going on among them. The striving for the unity of Christians has become more important than ever in the world of the twenty-first century with all challenges facing the future of the globe. In today's world there is no justifiable reason to maintain the old dichotomy between mission and unity, nor the division between ecumenical and evangelical Christians in Protestant Christianity. Christians simply cannot afford any longer to be divided among themselves. They are called to live in peace with each other and with all people of good will. An interreligious dimension has always been part of authentic Christian witness, and it is becoming more important than ever when common humanity is facing global crises. Christians need to face up to the challenges ahead of them with the others. If Christians want to be credible in their common witness in a world in crisis, they can no longer afford to maintain old divisions. "How can we, unreconciled to one another, proclaim one reconciliation for the world?"[44] Christians are one and they need to show that being reconciled and liberated by the grace of God, they can love each other (John 13:34–35). Loving one another is a powerful Christian witness because it shows concretely that Christians are one. Their witness to Christ becomes credible and gives hope to others.

---

43. Cameron, *Lausanne Legacy*, 147 (Part IID, 3).
44. Newbigin, *One Body One Gospel One World*, 54.

11

The Hope We Need to Imagine

THE IMC CENTENARY STUDY process out of which the idea for this book grew, happened during the COVID-19 pandemic. The online-based process linked researchers from all over the globe, sharing fears and hopes in a world on hold, joining in mourning the death of friends and celebrating life, but experiencing how differently such a global event hits the lives of people. This book has been written out of a deep awareness that many have been crushed and broken by conflicts, by poverty, by ecological disaster, even before the pandemic hit. We know that, for them, any talk of hope might very well seem hollow, facile or delusional. Yet our attempt to address today's multi-faceted crisis by mining a hundred years of thinking about ecumenical mission brings us, in the end, to the question of hope.

Such is our divided world that there are some contexts where a majority of people live in security and comfort. However, in our globalized world, events which seem to be far away polarize people in social media and even on the streets in front of our houses, challenging us to discern our involvement in these conflicts. The current operation of the global economy channels the lion's share of the available resources to a relatively small elite who can use these resources to ensure their own comfort and protect themselves from any threat of disturbance. This has been uncomfortably brought home, for example, by Michael Glazer's award-winning movie, *The Zone of Interest*.[1] He portrays the comfortable bourgeois life of the family of the commandant of the Auschwitz concentration camp whose home was

---

1. Klein, "Zone of Interest."

immediately adjacent to the camp. What happened, according to Glazer, is that "genocide became ambient to their lives."[2]

It is clear that questions raised by the film are less about what happened then and more about what is happening now. Are we continuing to create a world where some live in comfort and affluence while unspeakable horrors are inflicted on others? Such a situation is a scandal so far as the ecumenical vision is concerned. Key to its outlook is solidarity with the most vulnerable and the most injured. It insists on assessing the situation from the perspective of the most marginalized. This means coming to terms with the realities of our time, however painful they might be, and with our involvement in it. Hence a good part of this book has been devoted to exposing the death-dealing forces that bring privation, suffering, and death to many. We hope we have made it clear that, on our analysis, the world community needs to take a radically different direction from the one it is currently following.

Analysis, however, might not be enough. We noted at the outset that one particular dimension of today's crisis is that it raises doubts about the capacity of reason itself to overcome the crises. This is reflected in the term "hyper-complexity" which underscores the interconnected, multidimensional nature and scale of the crises facing the world today. It is emphasized here again to indicate the scale of the challenges, but even more importantly, to remind us that human action is limited for at least two reasons. One is that we are where we are today not as the result of a strategy even though the neoliberal capitalism is a major and dominant driver. We are where we are as the combined result of actions and single factors forming up to systems and their interactions, feedback loops, and unintended side effects. Sciences yield understanding of some of them but for the same reason it is not always clear which future action will have which effect and how the different possibilities will interact. The other obvious reason is that conflicting interests of different groups in the situations and conflicting ideas about how to solve the problems are part of the crises, deepening and accelerating them.

The fighting and killing in wars such as in Ukraine or armed conflicts such as in the Middle East can perhaps be stopped—but the conflicts are so deep and the interests of the fighting parties and their diverse allies so opposed that it seems almost impossible to find a solution that will allow peaceful coexistence in the near future. A similar observation can be made

---

2. Klein, "Zone of Interest," para. 12.

about the debates on the climate crises. There are still those who refuse to accept the imminent threat of climate change. But the bigger arguments are about how to avoid reaching the tipping point. Is it through more technology, which is not yet scalable to the extent that it will make a difference? Or is the only possible way out to change a lifestyle based on the depletion of resources through consumption? What consequences do both proposed solutions have in a world divided by the scandalous gap in wealth and in access to resources? In the attempt to become more green, the industrial nations started to run for rare earths, planning to ravage the last reserves like the deep sea mineral fields.

The dramatic changes in climate do affect all—even though the extent of our contributions to the causes varies dramatically. In 2024, the Earth overshoot day was August 1. Overshoot day means that from this day on we are "living on credit at the expense of future generations." However, people do that to different degrees in different countries. In the USA it was March 14, in Germany May 2. In the United Kingdom it was June 1, in Finland April 12, whereas in the Solomon Islands it was November 27.[3] Any solution will have to take account of the hyper-complexity of the problem indicated by how differently the same issue affects people in the different contexts. Or do we give up because of the excessive consumption of resources of one part of the world we have already crossed the tipping points and today's calamities will accompany us forever?

The COVID-19 pandemic is another good example of such hyper-complex interdependencies. The zoonosis of a virus from animals to humans is the result of humans constantly crossing into the plant and animal sphere. The interconnectedness of the world through just-in-time transport chains and easy traveling allowed the virus to spread with incredible speed and to kill. The restrictions imposed to stop the pandemic brought consumption to a near standstill by disrupting the supply chain and putting life on hold. In the pandemic we observed action groups who denied the scientific knowledge informing political decisions. Instead, they championed so-called alternative truths or, in other words, fake news, drawing on conspiracy theories to explain the events as an orchestrated campaign.[4] The fight against the pandemic was also a fight of worldviews and political models. On the other hand, the development of vaccines and some of the coordinated efforts which eventually stopped the pandemic are a good

---

3. "Earth Overshoot Day."
4. See Morsello, "'This Is the Real Face of Covid-19!'" and Klein, *Doppelganger*.

example of what humanity can achieve when it unites—but also, how vested interests stopped the sharing of the medicine that was available.

Such hyper-complexities present a formidable challenge to mission, requiring a reassessment of theological underpinnings and strategies. In face of the challenges that meet us at this moment, this book proposes a retrieval and redeployment of the ecumenical understanding of mission that developed from 1910 onwards. "Ecumenical," admittedly, is a slippery word and is often used simply as a term to describe churches being friendly to each other. This in itself is not to be underestimated—the Edinburgh 1910 World Missionary Conference proved to be a watershed as churches abandoned attitudes of suspicion and competition to think instead of cooperation and unity. But the ecumenical vision goes much further. It prompts us to think of mission in terms of "the whole inhabited earth," with no one excluded and no issues off limits. It does not stop when it has forged greater mutual understanding among different streams of Christian tradition but goes further to reach out to all communities of faith or no-faith, building relationships of mutual respect and seeking to make common cause in meeting contemporary challenges. Nor does it stop when it has enabled churches to reach a greater shared understanding of core Christian beliefs such as baptism or justification. The ecumenical vision is one that is ready to go out to counter all forces that make for death and to champion those that make for life.

The ecumenical understanding of mission is therefore one that is oriented to engage with issues such as those raised in this book, surveying some dimensions of our global context in the mid-2020s. As authors, we are united in appreciating and participating in the Christian tradition of faith and worship. However, we write to resist any sectarian or escapist turn in Christianity, which could be serious temptations in a bewildering and overwhelming situation. Religion seems to be particularly prone to the temptation to take the form of a comforting escape from unbearably harsh and painful realities. How could we grudge some measure of consolation to those who have faced great affliction? On the other hand, we see how religion is used by extremists to mobilize people. Neither the quietist nor the extremist expressions exhaust the richness of religious traditions. We argue that religious traditions are far more complex than such expressions which admittedly can be identified in many of our public spaces. Religion is a hyper-complex phenomenon starting with the never-ending debate about how to define what religion is, or what to include into an analysis of living religious tradition. Taking a Christian position within this spectrum, we claim that theology is in itself as a reflective practice hyper-complex. It is able to relate to science, ethics, politics, and to mobilize people, strengthen a practice of consoling individuals and groups, resilience, and supporting to cope with trauma-related stress. It empowers a communion that will help and support and transcend the thinking in ethnic or tribalist identities.

We find evidence of such practices and reflection in the history of ecumenical mission, formed in times of crisis and engaging with the crises of its times from a Christian position. The ecumenical vision formed in these periods will never allow us to rest content with consoling ourselves. It compels us to face the world situation, however distressing it might be, in the conviction that this is a world loved by God, renewed by Christ, and indwelt by the Holy Spirit and that we as Christians witness to these realities. We aim to champion the ecumenical vision, which inspires us to build bridges with others and to confront the acute challenges facing our world community at this time. It is precisely because of the hyper-complexity of these challenges that today the ecumenical understanding of mission is needed more than ever.

LEARNING FROM ECUMENICAL EXPERIENCE

At the heart of the ecumenical vision as we mined it is the concept of hope, which provides a lens through which mission can be both imagined and enacted in the midst of daunting challenges. In this context, hope serves as a critical theological resource that motivates and sustains mission work. It acknowledges the reality of suffering and the complexity of global problems, but insists on the possibility of transformation. It is an approach which recognizes the limitation of human activity and at the same time transcends those limits by opening a new horizon. Mission in hope becomes an act of participation in God's ongoing work of renewal, driven by hope for the kingdom already but not yet fully realized "through the Holy Spirit who affirms the vision of the reign of God, 'Behold, I create new heavens and a new earth!' (Isa 65:17). We commit ourselves together in humility and hope to the mission of God, who recreates all and reconciles all."[5]

The ecumenical movement was born out of hope—both the over-optimistic expectations of the Edinburgh 1910 World Missionary Conference

---

5. Keum, *Together Towards Life*, §112. See the chapter "People of Hope" in Ross, *Mission Rediscovered*, 111–16.

and the more chastened outlook of the International Missionary Council, formed in 1921 in the aftermath of the First World War. In the search for missionary cooperation and a future in which the Christian message could contribute to bring about transformation there was hope for unity, hope for transformation, and hope for a world more fully in line with the values of the gospel. After the devastation of the Second World War, a further ecumenical development was the formation of the World Council of Churches (WCC) in 1948. At its second Assembly held at Evanston, Illinois, in 1954, it explicitly struck the note of hope with the theme "Christ—the Hope of the World."[6] The assembly's focus on hope was not just about nurturing an optimistic outlook but was deeply rooted in the Christian understanding of hope as a transformative power that drives the church's engagement with the world, in the midst of all our differences. This hope is not passive but is active and engaged, looking towards the future with a vision of Christ's kingdom as a guiding light for action in the present. The theme served as a reminder that Christian hope is anchored in the person and work of Christ, offering a foundation for the church's witness and service in a world marked by uncertainty and despair.

After the earlier decades of crises, the theme of hope corresponded well to the optimistic feeling in the second half of the twentieth century of being in new times of rapid social change or in revolutionary times[7] which led to the hope that Christ "makes all things new."[8] These strands resonated in different ways with the outstanding theologians of the time like Rubem Alves, Gustavo Gutiérrez, and Jürgen Moltmann. These different theologians interacted in fora of the ecumenical movement at the time such as the 1966 conference *Christians in the Technical and Social Revolutions of our Time*.[9]

The multi-talented Brazilian reformed theologian Rubem Alves (1933–2014) was an influential and eclectic thinker in Latin America and played an important role in the development of Liberation Theology. In his *Theology of Human Hope* (1969) hope is a vital, driving force that compels individuals to seek change and transformation in their lives and societies.

6. *Evanston Report*.

7. *Christians in the Technical and Social Revolutions of our Time*. See already the title of the 1947 IMC conference *Renewal and Advance*.

8. Goodall, *Uppsala Report 1968*.

9. In its first meeting in 1969 Gutiérrez gave a lecture which foreshadowed his seminal book "Theology of Liberation" and Moltmann submitted a paper without attending. See Mateus, "On Moltmann, Sodepax and the Ecumenical Origins of Liberation Theology."

For Alves, hope is deeply connected to the divine promise of a better future of a God who opts for the marginalized. The eschatological perspective provides a theological foundation for hope which opens the imagination to an alternative to the experience of injustice and oppression, leading to an active commitment to transforming the present reality. It is a hope that despite present sufferings, a new creation and human flourishing is possible and is being brought about by God.[10]

In a similar line, the Peruvian Catholic theologian Gustavo Gutiérrez (*1928) suggested that authentic hope can be found through a preferential option for the poor, which implies a commitment to the struggles of the marginalized and oppressed. For him, God's liberating presence is encountered in the struggle for justice. It is the anticipation and active work towards a future where justice and peace prevail. For Gutiérrez, hope is manifested through praxis, the cycle of action and reflection that seeks to transform the world in accordance with God's kingdom, guided by the eschatological vision of what the world should be according to God's justice.[11]

Reformed theologian Jürgen Moltmann of Germany (1926–2024) anchored his theology in the promise of hope,[12] based on the resurrection of Jesus Christ. This hope in God's future acts as a transformative force in the present, challenging Christians to engage actively with the world in anticipation of the coming of God's kingdom. Moltmann drew heavily on the concept of eschatology, not as a distant or abstract future but as a reality that has already begun with the resurrection of Jesus. Belonging to the generation struck by war and in whose time the Holocaust was committed, he spoke of the "crucified God" to suggest that God's future-oriented hope is born out of the depths of divine suffering and solidarity with human suffering. This is the foundation of hope, as it assures believers of God's ultimate victory over death and suffering. It orients Christian life and action towards the future fulfillment of God's promises, when justice, peace, and life will triumph over injustice, violence, and death.

In retrospect, it seems that hope emerged as a theme when there was a widespread sense that Christian engagement with the world—understood in terms of holistic mission—contributed to its positive development towards a just future by revolution and liberation.[13] One of the surprising

---

10. Alves, *Theology of Human Hope*, originally published in 1969.

11. Gutiérrez, *Theology of Liberation*, originally published in 1971.

12. Moltmann, *Theology of Hope*, originally published in 1964.

13. For a more recent discussion on hope see for example van Den Heuvel, *Historical and Multidisciplinary Perspectives on Hope*.

aspects of studying the history of the mission and the ecumenical movement in relation to hope is to realize that mission always theologized in the context of crises and has itself always been a risky enterprise. The need to reflect on mission in times of crisis is not new to the discipline and recognition that mission is itself in crisis is not new either. Since mission is joining in God's mission it participates in the *krisis* that is God's coming into this world, expressed in the tension between the "already" and "yet to come."

Theologically, hope is the eschatological moment when the world opens up to God's activity breaking into this world. The emergence of hope seems to have been underpinned by a shift from a more Christological understanding of mission,[14] which challenged Christians to engage, to a more trinitarian understanding of mission, following the concept of *missio Dei*. A trinitarian framework makes us aware that the key terms of the ecumenical movement can be interpreted as referring to and expressing the inner *oikonomia* of salvation of God—Father, Son, and Holy Spirit. Second Corinthians 5:17 summarizes it well: "Therefore, if anyone is in Christ, the new creation has come: The old has gone, the new is here!" Here hope is understood as following the trinitarian movement from the salvation achieved in Christ, the Spirit being present and at work in the world and God father as creator and recreator of the broken creation.

ECUMENICAL MISSION MEANS HOPE

How can we sustain this conviction when so much of the evidence runs counter to it, when our world looks abandoned and doomed? The ecumenical vision does not entail any false consciousness that fails to reckon with reality. Instead, it offers a deeply realistic form of hope, one that reckons with painful adversities yet remains convinced that these do not have the last word. As Václav Havel remarked, "Hope is not prognostication. It is an orientation of the spirit, an orientation of the heart; it transcends the world that is immediately experienced, and is anchored somewhere beyond its horizons." Hope is "an ability to work for something because it is good, not just because it stands a chance to succeed."[15]

When we think of hope in such a Christian perspective, it brings us immediately to eschatology—the question of our final destiny. The

---

14. This can be identified in the motto of doing mission in Christ's way as expounded in the 1982 WCC mission statement "Mission and Evangelism."

15. Cited in Solnit, *Hope in the Dark*, 11.

eschatological fulfillment is often thought to refer to the "last things" (τo ἔσχατον) and is connected to resurrection, last judgment, heaven, and hell in dogmatic theology. Yet it is *not only* about future, because it is "already," and even if it is *also* in the future, it is "not yet." "Only by taking transcendence in eschatology seriously can Christian hope envisage the past as redeemed, not just left behind, and integrate the future of the individual, body and soul, with the future of the world, historical and cosmological."[16]

This eschatological aspect is intrinsically linked to soteriology—the doctrine of salvation. Since God has overcome death in Christ, we believe that something can happen that has not yet happened before, even before the last days.[17] "Hope for the fulfillment of God's promises of salvation from sin, and victory over evil, is characterized by a critique of the present (a negation of the negative) and the anticipation of a promised novum. It thus leads to inspiration, expectation and resistance, but also to patience and perseverance."[18]

Because the eternal God is the final goal of creation, mission reminds us of "eternal life" referring to a participation in the eternal life of God. There is nothing imperfect in God, so the divine fullness enables mortal creatures to transcend the mortality of this world. The eastern tradition of Christianity has used the term "divinization" (*theosis*).[19] Creatures will not literally become God, but they can be included within the divine life. This is where mission starts, and this is where it ends. The "Arusha Call to Discipleship," adopted by the WCC Conference on World Mission and Evangelism in 2018, refers to this profound theological concept: "In what the church's early theologians called 'theosis' or deification, we share God's grace by sharing God's mission."[20]

The missionary God, who has created the world, has the final responsibility and charge of the world. Because it is God, not a human being, who is in charge, there are no limits to the possibilities. God showed creative divine power in Jesus's resurrection. Mission in hope intentionally and creatively keeps this good future of the world in its view. It also motivates and encourages missionary disciples to move on and work for the unity of church and mission. We can confidently affirm that "it is God who gives

---

16. Bauckham, "Eschatology," 313.
17. Conradie, "In Search of a Vision of Hope for a New Century," 9.
18. Conradie, "In Search of a Vision of Hope for a New Century," 18.
19. See, e.g., Felmy, "Vergöttlichung."
20. "Arusha Call to Discipleship," 2.

unity to history and reveals himself in history. This is possible only if history moves towards an end."[21] Mission and church are witnesses to this unity, the final destiny: community with God.

In the Bible the forthcoming world is often depicted in apocalyptic imagery, flourishing currently in literature and movies. The religious scholar Alexander-Kenneth Nagel writes that in an apocalyptic semantics the narrator acts in a compressed in-between time, marking the beginning of the end of the world. Nagel ties this to apocalyptic pragmatics or rhetoric, that is, what actions such narratives are meant to inspire.[22] Applying this to Christian hope, it suggests that hope maintains the present open to the future, akin to how the horizon keeps space open. At this moment, the future reminds the present that things are transient, urging recognition of our God given gifts (*charismata*) and human abilities, but also of our limitations. We are not the ones to build his kingdom to come as heaven on earth. As earthly creatures we are not the opposite to a sphere called nature, but part of a much more comprehensive whole that theology conceptualizes as creation, which we will never fully comprehend. Believing in God as the creator of heaven and earth tells us as humans, first of all, that it is not us who are creating the world.

This should caution us to pay attention to the question of how we "read" the state of our world, in the mirror of the Gospels and the biblical apocalyptic. In the context of our time, we need to caution against the temptations of modern end-time images such as the climate crisis or the pandemics as apocalyptic events, or the coming of an artificial superintelligence bringing the end of humankind. The narratives we construct around such crises significantly influence our collective imagination concerning potential solutions. Christians do not know what will happen between now and the end. But they believe that in the end there will be not wars, conflicts, climate change, poverty, famine or natural disasters, but God—God will be all in all (1 Cor 15:28) and that human destiny is unavoidably theocentric. In the end, the human being will be in immediate relationship with God, which can be called the "vision of God," and the vision of God "will include seeing God in all things, participating in the transparently and joyously theocentric world of creation indwelt by God."[23] In this vision, the power of maybe the most creative feature of the human is decisive, i.e., the

---

21. Macquarrie, "Figure of Jesus Christ in Contemporary Christianity," 926.

22. Nagel, "Die Gegenwart der Endzeit," 181–82.

23. Bauckham, "Eschatology," 320.

power of imagination, which includes "the ability to detach oneself from one's own situation and to transpose oneself into any other position one might choose."[24] Without knowing what this will look like, the *eschaton* avoids a closure of the present by keeping the imagination open for possible futures. The risky moment in that process is that decisions need to be taken in order to break through the given and that the choice in favor of one path necessarily excludes other possible paths.

FRAMEWORK FOR MISSION: HOPE-BASED ACTION

A vital contribution to the creation of meaningful hope was made by the WCC World Mission Conference held at Athens in 2005. In face of a world marked by conflict, woundedness, and brokenness, it took up the theme of mission as reconciliation. One important step it took was to invoke an eschatological horizon that transcends conflict, even if overcoming it seems unlikely in the conflict-ridden present. As it recognized how wounded is our world, the Athens Conference focused on the role of the local church congregation (see ch. 7 in this book). Emphasizing reconciliation brought awareness of the power of congregations to become spaces of survival and healing under horrible circumstances while working for a better future. It also demonstrated the capacity of congregations to cope with the effects after the catastrophes when victims and perpetrator lived next to each other.[25]

The challenge of this perspective of reconciliation is that those who dare to reconcile become "new" in order to reconcile with others, and that they anchor themselves in this vision already in the midst of struggles and conflict. It is a hope, borne by the love of Christ, to shape the future because the present has become unbearable.

In doing so, we can be guided by the belief that whatever we can do will be of no use unless the Spirit of God heals and transforms the world—we should not lose sight of these dimensions of God's love in our mission. All Christian reflection and action are enfolded in God's love and the promise simultaneously shows the limits of all human endeavor. This is the gift of reconciliation that God gives in the communion of Father, Son, and Holy Spirit.

This hope, anchored in the trinitarian *oikonomia* of Christ's resurrection and the promise of God's future, enables Christians and the church to

---

24. Pannenberg, *What Is Man?*, 25.
25. Cases include Rwanda, South Africa, or the Balkans after the wars of the 1990s.

engage the crises with courage and creativity. Being reconciled with God through God offers the gift of justification. We are justified by faith, not by deeds or achievements, and this offers a crucial corrective to human hubris. Guided by the principle of justification by faith, mission work proceeds with humility, acknowledging that, while human efforts are indispensable, they are ultimately enfolded into God's transformative action.

Hope not only sustains mission in the face of daunting challenges but also shapes its character, orienting it towards the kingdom of God, where justice, peace, and the integrity of creation will be fully realized. In this eschatological vision, the kingdom of God is a definitive idea when it comes to understanding the meaning of mission.[26] Jesus preached about it and his prayer to God was that "your kingdom come" (Matt 6:10). Jesus's prayer is at the same time hope raising, humble, and confident—and future oriented.[27] There are no limits to this coming: it is spiritual, social, and political. Mission aims at flourishing communities, witnessing to the love of God and pointing to the willingness of Jesus Son of God and his followers to go an extra mile for everybody but in particular for those who are marginalized. A glimpse of God's kingdom can be heard and seen in Jesus's words at the synagogue of Nazareth (Luke 4:18–19).

On the level of engagement with the world, the eschatological vision challenges the notion that human efforts can fully resolve the crisis we face. It leads to a reorientation of mission around faith and hope, rather than around achievements and solutions. This reminds us that, while human action is necessary, it is ultimately God who redeems and renews. Mission, therefore, must be undertaken with humility, recognizing our limitations and the potential of unintended consequences in all our activity in a hypercomplex world. This approach does not lead to passivity but rather to a deeper reliance on God's grace and a commitment to faithful presence and action in the world.

When it comes to reason and reflection, we should be reminded that since we are part of the whole, at the current point in time, we can never take a perspective that encompasses the whole. The failure to recognize our limitation is in theology conceived of as sin: the striving for complete knowledge and the desire to be like God. Instead as a whole, the world

---

26. The following sentences follow Bauckham, "Eschatology," 320.

27. Pannenberg remarks: "Only the biblical promises have made the new thing of the future significant on the one hand and reliable on the other." Pannenberg, *What Is Man?*, 43.

appears to us as segmented into different spheres of reality, each understood in their own way.[28] This is reflected in the concept of hyper-complexity which requires us to acknowledge that crises such as climate change are not isolated challenges but are deeply interconnected. A missional response informed by a trinitarian theology of hope seeks to identify these connections and to address them. This approach prioritizes systemic change and long-term solutions over immediate results, grounded in the hope of God's future which encourages even in the face of the magnitude of the task and which supports congregations by a spirituality of patience even in the face of suffering that we meet on the way into an uncertain future.

Much of what we experience as the consequences of economic poverty, migration flows or the climate crisis has so far been part of human experience in the world. These are not calamities which now bring the end to an otherwise better world. What is new is the magnitude and the interplay of the phenomena that create a hyper-complex situation. Such an awareness encourages us to accept difficulties, challenges, and suffering as enduring elements of the present that is in the process of becoming the future. It avoids closing our minds against possible futures by despairing about how things are. This awareness orients the search for solutions and, above all, commitment to actions which have the power to change the situation.

Such reflection is promoted by *Together Towards Life* (TTL) (2012). On the basis of the pneumatological approach that the Spirit is the "true" missionary, mission is understood as a matter of discerning the signs of God's presence in the Spirit in this world and witnessing to the outpouring of the trinitarian dynamic within the life of God into God's creation. Hope in the God of life strengthens the power to remain and resist when we meet with intractable and heartbreaking situations of injustice that can often appear to leave us defeated. Faith can provoke a sense of urgency while at the same time recognizing the penultimate character of the contemporary struggle and returning to the ultimate vision for fresh inspiration and energy whenever this is needed. As Martin Luther King Jr. remarked, "We must accept finite disappointment, but never lose infinite hope."[29] In this way the ecumenical vision inspires the passionate urgency needed to engage the crises of our time while also imparting the staying power needed to overcome repeated disappointment. As the WCC "Arusha Conference Report" stated: "A spirituality of resilience is at the center of the theological

---

28. Gabriel, *Why the World Does Not Exist*.
29. Cited in Solnit, *Hope in the Dark*, xvi.

and missional formation for discipleship. It requires the formation of communities of Christians that are resilient in the face of injustice, that are humble and courageous in persistently challenging the unjust system."[30]

The hope that is inspired by the ecumenical vision is not just a wistful longing for things to be different from the way they are now. Rather, it is the engine that powers a movement for transformation, one that can engage the most ugly and dispiriting realities and can weather endless disappointments. It can do this because it is rooted and grounded in the triune God who loves the world in all its brokenness and whose mission is to make all things whole. To meet the hyper-complexity and traumatic impact of the global crisis that meets us today, we need the vision of the "larger Christ" that inspired the ecumenical movement in its origins.[31] Hope rises from the conviction that Christ's salvation is big enough, strong enough, deep enough to deliver us from the many-sided crisis that threatens to engulf us. Such hope gives us the confidence to go out to build the widest life-affirmative alliance we can, reaching out to apparently unlikely partners with the eye for the marginalized that was such a marked feature of Jesus's earthly ministry. Building walls to protect what we wrongly imagine to be our own safe space is a fatal strategy. Instead, it is time for a new ecumenical adventure, for an expansive outlook that brings the vision of faith to bear on our hyper-complex crisis and creates common ground on which a great diversity of allies can unite to confront every threat in the power of hope.

Mission in hope invites us to the adventure of walking together into a future that is believed to be changeable. As we have explained, we do not see Christians as the only agents of transformation but as those seeking allies. Such an approach encourages, especially when not all share the same faith, the promotion of values and attitudes, which do not allow mercy to fade and which work for justice, reconciliation, and peace, as a sign of Christian mission within a wider encounter and communion. This communion on the way can include all those who share the values and objectives mentioned above, even if they do not share the Christian motivation. In the communion of walking with the many in society, the witness of our faith becomes one of respect for the faith of others. The transforming power here would be openness to the action of God, who not only blesses lived engagement, but also includes it in God's eschatological promise. We are as Christians always on the way: the consummation is yet to come, but the

---

30. "Arusha Conference Report," 16.

31. International Missionary Council, *Addresses and Papers of John R. Mott*, 19–20.

Spirit is already transforming here and now what we experience and live, what we hope and believe.[32] Mission reminds believers that through the Spirit they participate in the new age to come but they do it in transforming the world, their context, where they are here and now. There is no direct jump from this moment to the future. In fact, humans seem to neglect the present as they mourn over the past and are afraid of the future.[33]

The framework for mission of hope led by the Spirit, we propose, can be summarized by several key orientations:

Creation Awareness

"We affirm that mission begins with God's act of creation and continues in re-creation, by the enlivening power of the Holy Spirit" (TTL, §102). It is high time to reflect more deeply on mission in the framework of a theology of creation and re-creation that transcends the anthropocentrism of traditional theology. We need to learn to understand better what it means to be a member in God's household. The climate crisis is not a crisis of the climate but of the living planet and our renewal is part of the renewal God promises for the whole of his creation.

Eschatological Orientation

Our mission needs to be grounded in the hope of God's promised future. In the line of theologies of hope, we emphasize that mission is first of all about reading the world in the light of the future the triune God envisages for creation and to engage with the world's crisis in the light of God's reign to come.

Personal Transformation

Mission starts with the outpouring of God's love (TTL, §2). The first who need to be transformed by it is none other than ourselves, recognizing that our human personhood is in crisis and that we find hope in the renewal of

---

32. "The Christological foundation of Christian hope must be supplemented by the work of the Holy Spirit in Christian experience." Bauckham, "Eschatology," 310.

33. Pannenberg, *What Is Man?*, 77.

our life promised by Jesus Christ. This renewal is expressed and strengthened in the communion of the saints, as the creed calls the church.

Humility and Reliance on God

Justification by faith means acknowledging our proneness to sin, our limitations, and our failures as humans prompting repentance and reconciliation. Such an awareness urges us to be open for others, for the diversity of people and the earth. Recognizing our limitations acknowledges the need for the wisdom and expertise of many. This must include the knowledge and expertise of people who are not Christians, even of those who oppose church and the Christian faith. In this we need to be guided by the Spirit, discerning the signs of God's presence in the Spirit in all contexts.

Holistic Engagement

Recognizing the interconnectedness of global crises and seeking solutions that are able to take these interconnections into consideration means avoiding simplistic solutions or those from which only a few profit. Instead of reactionary or desperate responses to the crisis that offer attractive but deceptive forms of religion, we call for a renewal of ecumenical witness that takes account of the full range and complexity of the crisis to offer a holistic witness.

Prophetic Witness

Recognizing that we are not in neutral environment but rather one in which powerful forces seek to shape history in favor of a dominant elite, we embrace a prophetic calling. This means a critique of current systems and practices that contribute to global crises, while pointing towards alternative, hope-filled ways of living.

Solidarity and Hospitality

Mission in hope emphasizes the importance of standing with those most affected by global crises, particularly those hardest hit by environmental degradation, violence, and poverty. Along the line of mission from the margins we need to learn to read the situation of the world from their perspective. This includes recognition of their wisdom and agency.

UNITY AS CATHOLICITY OF THE CHURCH

Mining the experience of the ecumenical movement, we believe that such a mission of hope in times of crisis is a matter of the Spirit and can mobilize many around the globe. We see signs of such engagement and churches are invited to join in unity. Such unity can be discovered in the framework of a mission in hope expressing the catholicity of the church.

The World Mission Conference in Salvador de Bahia (1996) stated, for example, that the "catholicity of a church is enhanced by the quality of the relationships it has with churches of other traditions and cultures." Local congregations are called "to be places of hope, providing spaces of safety and trust wherein different peoples can be embraced and affirmed, thus manifesting the inclusive love of God."[34] The WCC Assembly at Porto Alegre (2006) offered as a criterion on catholicity: "Each church is the Church catholic, but not the whole of it. Each church fulfils its catholicity when it is in communion with the other churches."[35]

The same can be said of mission: All Christians are in mission but none of us embodies the whole of it. Mission in unity is a matter of embarking on the adventure of journeying together towards a future that is believed to be transformable. This journey needs to be characterized by the understanding that God has a plan for the renewal of God's creation including humanity of which we as Christians know only small sparks. This encourages us to recognize that Christians will not be able to transform this world alone. Mission seeks, particularly in a world in which not all share the same faith, to live out values and attitudes as a sign of mission in encounters and accompaniment that do not allow mercy to fade and that work for justice, reconciliation, and peace. Such a journey can include all those who hold and share the values and goals mentioned, even if they do not share the reasons and motivation. The transformative aspect would be openness to the work of God, who not only blesses discipleship, but also places it under God's eschatological promise. The consummation is yet to

---

34. Duraisingh, *Called to One Hope*, 24.
35. Rivera-Pagán, *God, in Your Grace*, 257.

come, but the Spirit is already transforming what we have experienced and lived, what we hope and believe.[36]

Such is the depth of our contemporary crisis that we hesitate to suggest that it can be understood as an opportunity. The clouds above us are too dark and threatening, and the storms already too devastating in many contexts, to allow for any glib confidence that a positive outcome is on the horizon. Where we believe that the times of crisis do present an opportunity, however, is in regard to the retrieval and deployment of the ecumenical mission tradition. This, we hope, might be the distinctive contribution of this book. We have attempted to review this particular stream of thinking and action in a spirit of *metanoia* (repentance), recognizing that churches and missions have often been part of the problem. Yet we find that the unprecedented collaboration in the interests of Christian witness that developed during the twentieth century includes strands that hold enduring value and contemporary relevance. And we have been inspired by elements of renewal in thinking about mission—cherishing of life, environmental responsibility, action for justice, deepening of spirituality. Taken together, we propose that these open up a fresh vision of human identity and vocation that can be a vital resource in meeting the crisis of our times in hope.

36. See Biehl, "Prophetische Mission."

Authors

Marina Ngursangzeli Behera (DTh), originally from Mizoram, India, is a faculty member at the Oxford Centre for Mission Studies (OCMS), UK, and is responsible for the PhD stage research. She serves as editor of the peer-reviewed academic journal *Transformation* of OCMS. She has served at the United Theological College, Bangalore (2005–12) and held the chair of Ecumenical Missiology at the World Council of Churches' Ecumenical Institute, Bossey, Switzerland (2012–16), attached to the University of Geneva.

Michael Biehl (ThD) is an ordained pastor of the Evangelical Lutheran Church in the North (Germany), now retired. After pastoral ministry he served as Director of the Academy of Mission at the University of Hamburg (2001–12) and from 2012 to 2023 as executive secretary for mission studies and theological education at the Association of Protestant Missions and Churches in Germany (EMW). He taught mission studies, ecumenics, and religious studies at the Universities of Kiel and Hamburg (as adjunct lecturer) and is a research associate at the Faculty of Theology, University of Pretoria.

Risto Jukko (PhD, ThD, MEd) currently serves as Director of the Office for Global Mission of the Evangelical Lutheran Church of Finland. Between 2018 and 2022 he held the position of director of the Commission of World Mission and Evangelism of the World Council of Churches, based in Geneva, Switzerland. He is adjunct professor of ecumenics at the University of Helsinki and at the University of Eastern Finland.

Kenneth R. Ross (OBE, PhD) is professor of theology and dean of postgraduate studies at Zomba Theological University in Malawi. He is also extraordinary professor at the University of Pretoria in South Africa. Earlier he served as professor of theology at the University of Malawi, general secretary of the Church of Scotland Board of World Mission and chair of the Scotland Malawi Partnership. Currently he is series editor of the Edinburgh Companions to Global Christianity (Edinburgh University Press).

Bibliography

Adogame, Afe, et al., eds. *Engaging the World: Christian Communities in Contemporary Global Services*. Regnum Edinburgh Centenary Series 21. Oxford: Regnum, 2014.

Ahn, Kyo-Seong. "From Mission to Church and Beyond: The Metamorphosis of Post-Edinburgh Christianity." In *Edinburgh 2010: Mission Then and Now*, edited by David A. Kerr and Kenneth R. Ross, 74–84. Oxford: Regnum, 2009.

Alves, Rubem. *A Theology of Human Hope*. Washington, DC: Corpus, 1971.

Anderson, Perry. "Ever Closer Union?" *London Review of Books* 43 (2021) 25–34.

Anglican Communion. "Resolution 16.17: Joint Declaration on the Doctrine of Justification." https://www.anglicancommunion.org/structures/instruments-of-communion/acc/acc-16/resolutions.aspx#s17.

Antone, Hope, et al., eds. *Asian Handbook on Theological Education and Ecumenism*. Oxford: Regnum, 2013.

Apostolou, Nikolia. "Official Recognition for Ukrainian Church Roils Orthodox World." *National Catholic Reporter*, Jan. 2, 2019. https://www.ncronline.org/news/official-recognition-ukrainian-church-roils-orthodox-world.

"Arusha Call to Discipleship." In *Moving in the Spirit: Report of the World Council of Churches Conference on World Mission and Evangelism*, edited by Risto Jukko and Jooseop Keum, 2–4. Geneva: WCC, 2019.

"The Arusha Conference Report." In *Moving in the Spirit: Report of the World Council of Churches Conference on World Mission and Evangelism*, edited by Risto Jukko and Jooseop Keum, 5–19. Geneva: WCC, 2019.

Asamoah-Gyadu, J. Kwabena. "Reverse Evangelism: An African Pentecostal Perspective." In *Sharing Good News: Handbook on Evangelism in Europe*, edited by Gerrit Noort et al., 116–29. Geneva: WCC, 2017.

Ashworth, John, et al. *The Voice of the Voiceless: The Role of the Church in the Sudanese Civil War, 1983–2005*. Nairobi: Paulines, 2014.

Barreto, Raimundo C., Jr. "The International Missionary Council: From Lake Mohonk 1921 to New Delhi 1961." In *Together in the Mission of God: Jubilee Reflections on the International Missionary Council*, edited by Risto Jukko, 31–58. Geneva: WCC, 2022.

Barth, Karl. *Church Dogmatics*. 1/1: *The Doctrine of the Word of God*. London: T&T Clark, 2004.

———. "Die Theologie und die Mission in der Gegenwart." In *Theologische Fragen und Antworten*, 3:100–126. Zollikon-Zürich: Evangelischer Verlag, 1957.

Bartholomew, Patriarch. *Address by His All-Holiness Ecumenical Patriarch Bartholomew at the WCC Town-Hall Discussion on Interfaith Dialogue, Climate Change, and*

Bibliography

Refugee Displacement—at the Religious Leaders Unite for Climate Peace in Solidarity with Refugees. Ecumenical Center, Geneva, Switzerland, Dec. 12, 2023. https://www.oikoumene.org/resources/documents/address-by-his-all-holiness-ecumenical-patriarch-bartholomew-at-the-wcc-town-hall-discussion-on-interfaith-dialogue-climate-change-and-refugee-displacement.

———. "The Wonder of Creation and Ecology." In *Orthodox Perspectives on Mission*, edited by Petros Vassiliadis, 124–42. Oxford: Regnum, 2013.

Bassey, Nnimmo. *To Cook a Continent: Destructive Extraction and Climate Crisis in Africa*. Oxford: Pambazuka, 2012.

Bauckham, Richard. "Eschatology." In *The Oxford Handbook of Systematic Theology*, edited by John Webster et al., 306–22. Oxford: Oxford University Press, 2007.

Bearing Fruit: Implications of the 2010 Reconciliation Between Lutherans and Mennonites/Anabaptists Report of the Lutheran World Federation Task Force to Follow Up the "Mennonite Action" at the LWF Eleventh Assembly in 2010. Geneva: Lutheran World Federation, 2016.

Bebbington, David W. *Evangelicalism in Modern Britain: A History from the 1730s to the 1980s*. London: Routledge, 1989.

Behera, Marina Ngursangzeli. "'Global North and Global South': The Significance and Meaning of These Terms for Our Understanding and Practice of Mission." *Studia Universitatis Babeş-Bolyai. Theologia Orthodoxa* 64 (2019) 29–38.

———. "Mission. Chapter 31." In *Critical Terms in Futures Studies*, edited by Heike Paul, 199–202. Basingstoke: Palgrave MacMillan, 2019.

———. "Mission in Northeast India in the Early 20th Century: A Perspective from the Global South on the Founding of the IMC in the Global North." In *A Hundred Years of Mission Cooperation: The Impact of the International Missionary Council 1921–2021*, edited by Risto Jukko, 71–87. Geneva: WCC, 2022.

———. "Mission in Word—and in Practice? The Commission on World Mission and Evangelism of the World Council of Churches." In *Together in the Mission of God: Jubilee Reflections on the International Missionary Council*, edited by Risto Jukko, 59–82. Geneva: WCC, 2022.

Bendor-Samuel, Paul. "Challenge and Realignment in the Protestant Cross-Cultural Mission Movement." *Transformation* 34 (2017) 267–81.

Bergmann, Sigurd, and Mika Vähäkangas, eds. *Contextual Theology: Skills and Practices of Liberating Faith*. New Critical Thinking in Religion, Theology and Biblical Studies. London: Routledge, 2021.

Bevans, Stephen B. *Community of Missionary Disciples: The Continuing Creation of the Church*. Maryknoll, NY: Orbis, 2024.

———. "From Edinburgh to Edinburgh: Toward a Missiology for a World Church." In *Mission After Christendom: Emergent Themes in Contemporary Mission*, edited by Ogbu U. Kalu et al., 1–11. Louisville: Westminster John Knox, 2010.

———. "Together Towards Life: Reflections on the World Council of Churches Mission Statement." *Verbum SVD* 56 (2015) 146–59.

———. "Transforming Discipleship: Missiological Reflections." *International Review of Mission* 105 (2016) 355–66.

———. "'Your Light Must Shine before Others' (Matt 5:16): Faithful and Creative Discipleship in a Wounded World. A Reflection on the 2024 SVD General Chapter Theme." *Verbum SVD* 64 (2023) 159–76.

Bibliography

Bevans, Stephen B., SVD, and Roger P. Schroeder. *Constants in Context: A Theology of Mission for Today*. Maryknoll, NY: Orbis, 2004.

———. *Prophetic Dialogue: Reflections on Christian Mission Today*. Maryknoll, NY: Orbis, 2011.

Bhakiaraj, Paul Joshua. "Christianity in South-Central Asia, 1910–2010." In *Atlas of Global Christianity*, edited by Todd M. Johnson and Kenneth R. Ross, 142–43. Edinburgh: Edinburgh University Press, 2009.

Biehl, Michael. "Is Europe Lost? African Reverse Evangelism in Germany." In *Evangelism: Perspectives from an African Context*, edited by Johannes Knoetze, 279–97. Wellington: Barnabas Academic, 2024.

———. "Prophetische Mission." *Ökumenische Rundschau* 70 (2021) 431–40.

———. "Religion, Development and Mission." In *Religion: Help or Hindrance to Development?*, edited by Kenneth Mtata, 97–119. LWF Documentation 58. Leipzig: Evang. Verlagsanstalt, 2013.

———. "The Study Process of the IMC Centenary." In *A Hundred Years of Mission Cooperation: The Impact of the International Missionary Council 1921–2021*, edited by Risto Jukko, 3–11. Geneva: WCC, 2022.

———. "Zur Zukunft des Christentums und der Ökumene in missionswissenschaftlicher Perspektive." In *Ökumene—überdacht: Reflexionen und Realitäten im Umbruch*, edited by Thomas Bremer and Maria Wernsmann, 276–300. Quaestiones disputatae 259. Freiburg/Br.: Herder, 2014.

Bosch, David J. *Transforming Mission: Paradigm Shifts in Theology of Mission*. Maryknoll, NY: Orbis, 1991.

Briggs, John, et al., eds. *A History of the Ecumenical Movement*. Vol. 3: *1968–2000*. Geneva: WCC, 2004.

Bushby, Helen. "Permacrisis Declared Collins Dictionary Word of the Year." BBC, Oct. 31, 2022. https://www.bbc.com/news/entertainment-arts-63458467.

Called to Transformation: Ecumenical Diakonia. World Council of Churches and ACT Alliance. Geneva: WCC, 2022.

Cameron, J. E. M., ed. *The Lausanne Legacy: Landmarks in Global Mission*. Peabody, MA: Hendrickson, 2016.

Campbell, Heidi A., ed. *The Distanced Church: Reflections on Doing Church Online*. Digital Religion Publications. https://oaktrust.library.tamu.edu/handle/1969.1/187891.

The Cape Town Commitment: A Confession of Faith and a Call to Action. The Third Lausanne Congress. https://lausanne.org/wp-content/uploads/2021/10/The-Cape-Town-Commitment-%E2%80%93-Pages-20-09-2021.pdf.

Carey, William. *An Enquiry into the Obligations of Christians, to Use Means for the Conversion of the Heathens*. London: Hodder & Stoughton, 1891.

Carrying the Gospel to All the Non-Christian World: Report of Commission I, World Missionary Conference, 1910. Edinburgh: Oliphant, Anderson & Ferrier, 1910.

Chiappa, Claudia. "War Looms for Europe, Warns Poland's Donald Tusk." *Politico*, Mar. 29, 2024. https://www.politico.eu/article/polish-prime-minister-donald-tusk-warns-europe-pre-war-era/.

Chomsky, Noam. *Who Rules the World?* London: Hamish Hamilton, 2016.

Christ's Love Moves the World to Reconciliation and Unity. Report of the World Council of Churches 11th Assembly, Karlsruhe, Germany, 2022. Geneva: WCC, 2023.

Christianity in Its Global Context, 1970–2020. Society, Religion, and Mission. South Hamilton: Center for the Study of Global Christianity, GCTS, 2013. https://www.

gordonconwell.edu/wp-content/uploads/sites/13/2019/04/2ChristianityinitsGlobal Context.pdf.

Christian Witness in a Multi-Religious World: Recommendations for Conduct. https://www.oikoumene.org/resources/documents/christian-witness-in-a-multi-religious-world.

Christians in the Technical and Social Revolutions of our Time. Official Report, World Conference on Church and Society. Geneva: WCC, 1967.

The Church in the Mission Field. Report of Commission II. World Missionary Conference, 1910. Edinburgh, London: Oliphant, Anderson & Ferrier, 1910.

Clarke, Matthew, and John Donnelly. "Learning from Missionaries: Lessons for Secular Development Practitioners." In *Engaging the World. Christian Communities in Contemporary Global Services*, edited by Afe Adogame et al., 169–83. Regnum Edinburgh Centenary Series 21. Oxford: Regnum, 2014.

Clements, Keith. *Faith on the Frontier: A Life of J. H. Oldham.* Edinburgh: T&T Clark, 1999.

Climate Change 2023: Synthesis Report. Contribution of Working Groups I, II and III to the Sixth Assessment Report of the Intergovernmental Panel on Climate Change. Edited by H. Lee and J. Romero. Geneva: IPCC, 2023.

Conradie, Ernst M. *The Earth in God's Economy: Creation, Salvation and Consummation in Ecological Perspective.* Studies in Religion and the Environment 10. Berlin: Lit, 2015.

———. "Environment." In *Ecumenical Missiology: Changing Landscapes and New Conceptions of Mission*, edited by Kenneth R. Ross et al., 320–30. Geneva: WCC, 2016.

———. "In Search of a Vision of Hope for a New Century." *Journal of Religion and Society* 1 (1999) 1–24.

Conway, Martin. "Under Public Scrutiny." In *A History of the Ecumenical Movement*, edited by John Briggs et al., 3:433–58. Geneva: WCC, 2004.

Crane, William H. "Editorial: Dropping the S." *International Review of Mission* 58 (1969) 141–44.

Crist, Meehan. "War in Ukraine." *London Review of Books* 44 (2022) 9.

De Wit, Hans, et al., eds. *Reading Through the Eyes of Another: Intercultural Reading of the Bible.* Elkhart, IA: Institute of Mennonite Studies, 2004.

Deleuze, Gilles, and Félix Guattari. *A Thousand Plateaus: Capitalism and Schizophrenia.* Minneapolis: University of Minnesota Press, 1987.

Denzinger, Heinrich. *Kompendium der Glaubensbekenntnisse und kirchlichen Lehrentscheidungen. Lateinisch—Deutsch.* Edited by Peter Hünermann. Freiburg: Herder, 2005.

Douglas, J. D., ed. *Let the Earth Hear His Voice: International Congress on World Evangelization, Lausanne, Switzerland.* Minneapolis: World Wide, 1975.

Dowsett, Rose, et. al., eds. *Evangelisation and Diaconia in Context.* Regnum Edinburgh Centenary Series 32. Oxford: Regnum, 2015.

Drønen, Tomas Sundnes. "Christian Mission and International Development." In *The Oxford Handbook of Mission Studies*, edited by Kirsteen Kim et al., 257–73. Oxford: Oxford University Press, 2022.

Duraisingh, Christopher, ed. *Called to One Hope: The Gospel in Diverse Cultures.* Geneva: WCC, 1998.

"Earth Overshoot Day." https://www.genevaenvironmentnetwork.org/resources/updates/earth-overshoot-day/#scroll-nav__2.

BIBLIOGRAPHY

Education in Relation to the Christianisation of National Life. Report of Commission III, World Missionary Conference, 1910. Edinburgh, London: Oliphant, Anderson & Ferrier, n.d.

The Evanston Report. The Second Assembly of the World Council of Churches 1954. London: SCM, 1955.

Felmy, Karl Christian. "Vergöttlichung." In *Religion in Geschichte und Gegenwart. Handwörterbuch für Theologie und Religionswissenschaft*, edited by Hans Dieter Betz et al., 8:1008. Tübingen: Mohr Siebeck, 2005.

Fey, Harold C., ed. *A History of the Ecumenical Movement*. Vol. 2: *1948–1968*. Geneva: WCC, 2004.

Forrester, Duncan B. *Apocalypse Now? Reflections on Faith in a Time of Terror*. Aldershot: Ashgate, 2005.

Francis, Pope. *Evangelii Gaudium. Apostolic Exhortation to the Bishops, Clergy, Consecrated Persons and the Lay Faithful on the Proclamation of the Gospel in Today's World*. Rome: Vatican, 2013. https://www.vatican.va/content/francesco/en/apost_exhortations/documents/papa-francesco_esortazione-ap_20131124_evangelii-gaudium.html.

———. *Laudate Deum: Apostolic Exhortation to All People of Good Will on the Climate Crisis*. Rome: Vatican, 2023. https://www.vatican.va/content/francesco/en/apost_exhortations/documents/20231004-laudate-deum.html.

———. *Laudato Si': Encyclical Letter On Care for Our Common Home*. Rome: Vatican, 2015. https://www.vatican.va/content/francesco/en/encyclicals/documents/papa-francesco_20150524_enciclica-laudato-si.html.

Frankopan, Peter. *The Earth Transformed: An Untold Story*. London: Bloomsbury, 2023.

Gabriel, Markus. *Why the World Does Not Exist*. Hoboken, NJ: Wiley & Sons, 2017.

Gaillardetz, Richard. "Implementing Synodality: Reflections on Two Recent Contributions." *Worship* 95 (2021) 100–107.

Global Methodist Church. "Launch Information." https://globalmethodist.org/launch-information/.

Global Survey on Theological Education. "Summary of Main Findings for World Council of Churches 10th Assembly, Busan, October 30–November 8 2013." https://www.oikoumene.org/resources/documents/global-survey-on-theological-education.

Goodall, Norman, ed. *The Uppsala Report 1968. Official Report of the Fourth Assembly of the World Council of Churches Uppsala July 4–20, 1968*. Geneva: WCC, 1968.

Greschat, Martin. *Der Erste Weltkrieg und die Christenheit: Ein globaler Überblick*. Stuttgart: Kohlhammer, 2014.

Gros, Jeffrey FSC, et al., eds. *Growth in Agreement II: Reports and Agreed Statements of Ecumenical Conversations on a World Level, 1982–1998*. Geneva: WCC, 2000.

Gunda, Masiiwa Ragies. "Rethinking Development in Africa and the Role of Religion." In *Religion and Development in Africa*, edited by Ezra Chitando et al., 38–57. Bible in Africa Studies 25. Exploring Religion in Africa 4. Bamberg: University of Bamberg Press, 2020.

Gutiérrez, Gustavo, *A Theology of Liberation: History, Politics, and Salvation*. 50th Anniversary Edition. Maryknoll, NY: Orbis, 2023.

Hardiman, David, "Introduction." In *Healing Bodies, Saving Souls: Medical Missions in Asia and Africa*, edited by David Hardiman, 1–57. The Wellcome Series in the History of Medicine. Amsterdam: Editions Rodopi B.V., 2006.

Hartenstein, Karl. *Die Mission als theologisches Problem*. Berlin: Furche Verlag, 1933.

The Henley Passport Index. https://www.henleyglobal.com/passport-index.

BIBLIOGRAPHY

Hilberat, Bernd Jochen. "Filioque II. Systematisch-theologisch." In *Lexikon für Theologie und Kirche, Dritter Band*, edited by Walter Kasper, 1280. Freiburg: Herder, 2006.

In Gottes Lehre. Theologische Ausbildung weltweit. Jahresbericht 2018–19. Hamburg: EMW, 2019. https://mission-weltweit.de/assets/content/doc/themen/In-Gottes-Lehre_EMW-Jahresbericht_18-19.pdf.

Inayatullah, Sohail. "Six Pillars: Futures Thinking for Transforming." *Foresight* 10 (2008) 4–21.

Intergovernmental Panel on Climate Change (IPCC). "Summary for Policymakers." In *Climate Change 2023: Synthesis Report. Contribution of Working Groups I, II and III to the Sixth Assessment Report of the Intergovernmental Panel on Climate Change*, edited by H. Lee and J. Romero, 1–34. Geneva: IPCC, 2023. https://www.ipcc.ch/report/ar6/syr/downloads/report/IPCC_AR6_SYR_FullVolume.pdf.

The International Missionary Council. *Addresses and Papers of John R. Mott*. Vol. 5. New York: Association, 1947.

International Organization for Migration. *World Migration Report 2022*. Geneva: IOM, 2022. https://worldmigrationreport.iom.int/wmr-2022-interactive/.

Istavridis, Vasil T. "The Orthodox Churches in the Ecumenical Movement 1948–1968." In *A History of the Ecumenical Movement*, edited by Harold C. Fey, 2:289–309. Geneva: WCC, 2004.

Jamir, Chongpongmeren, and H. Lalrinthanga, eds. *Transformative Rethinking: Christian Mission and Cooperation in a Multireligious Indian Society*. International Missionary Council Centenary Series. Oxford: Regnum, 2024.

Johnson, Todd M., and Kenneth R. Ross, eds. *Atlas of Global Christianity 1910–2020*. Edinburgh: Edinburgh University Press, 2009.

Joint Catholic-Lutheran Commemoration of The Reformation. "Joint Ecumenical Commemoration." https://www.lund2016.net/about_1.html.

Joint Declaration on the Doctrine of Justification. https://lutheranworld.org/sites/default/files/Joint%20Declaration%20on%20the%20Doctrine%20of%20Justification.pdf.

Joshua Project. "What Is the 10/40 Window?" https://joshuaproject.net/resources/articles/10_40_window.

Jukko, Risto, ed. *Conference on World Mission and Evangelism, 2018*. Complete Digital Edition of the Arusha Report. Geneva: WCC, 2019. https://www.oikoumene.org/sites/default/files/2020-10/Digital%20Edition_Arusha%20Report_20052019_compressed.pdf.

———. "The Doctrine of the Trinity and the Theology of Religions in Postmodern Society." In *Deepening Faith, Hope and Love in Relations with Neighbors of Other Faiths*, edited by Simone Sinn, 147–56. Geneva: Lutheran World Federation, 2008.

———, ed. *The Future of Mission Cooperation: The Living Legacy of the International Missionary Council*. Geneva: WCC, 2022.

———, ed. *A Hundred Years of Mission Cooperation: The Impact of the International Missionary Council 1921–2021*. Geneva: WCC, 2022.

———. "Toward Prophetic Missionary Discipleship." In *Together in the Mission of God: Jubilee Reflections on the International Missionary Council*, edited by Risto Jukko, 295–311. Geneva: WCC, 2022.

———, ed. *Together in the Mission of God: Jubilee Reflections on the International Missionary Council*. Geneva: WCC, 2022.

Jukko, Risto, and Jooseop Keum, eds. *Moving in the Spirit: Report of the World Council of Churches Conference on World Mission and Evangelism*. Geneva: WCC, 2019.

Bibliography

Jun, Guichun. "Mission in the Age of Digitalization: Metaverse, Metamodernism, and Metanarrative." In *Together in the Mission of God: Jubilee Reflections on the International Missionary Council*, edited by Risto Jukko, 241–60. Geneva: WCC, 2022.

Just Peace Companion. "Guide Our Feet Into the Way of Peace" (Luke 1:79). 2nd ed. Geneva: WCC, 2012.

Kairos for Creation. *Confessing Hope for the Earth: The "Wuppertal Call." Contributions and Recommendations from an International Conference on Eco-Theology and Ethics of Sustainability, Wuppertal, Germany, 16–19 June 2019*. Edited by Louk Adrianos et al. For Human Rights 20. Solingen: Foedus, 2019.

Kaiser, Andrew T. "Field Workers and Mission Leaders in Tension: Practical Ecumenism in the Shanxi Mission." In *Ecumenism and Independency in World Christianity. Historical Studies in Honour of Brian Stanley*, edited by Alexander Chow and Emma Wild-Wood, 177–94. Theology and Mission in World Christianity 15. Leiden: Brill, 2020.

Kakutani, Michiko. *The Great Wave: The Era of Radical Disruption and the Rise of the Outsider*. New York: Crown, 2024.

Kalaitzidis, Pantelis, et al., eds. *Orthodox Handbook for Teaching Ecumenism*. Oxford: Regnum, 2013.

Kaldor, Mary. *New and Old Wars: Organized Violence in a Global Era*. Stanford: Stanford University Press, 2012.

Kalu, Ogbu U. "To Hang a Ladder in the Air: An African Assessment." In *Edinburgh 2010. Mission Then and Now*, edited by David A. Kerr and Kenneth R. Ross, 91–104. Regnum Studies in Mission. Oxford: Regnum, 2009.

Kalu, Ogbu U., et al., eds. *Mission after Christendom: Emergent Themes in Contemporary Mission*. Louisville: Westminster John Knox, 2010.

Kaunda, Chammah J. *"Imagining a Just and Equitable African Christian Community": A Critical Analysis of the Contribution of Theological Education Fund/Ecumenical Theological Education (1910–2012)*. Pietermaritzburg: School of Religion, 2013.

Kern, Lisa, and Lester Edwin J. Ruiz. "The Global Forum of Theological Educators Holds Second Meeting in Crete." https://www.ats.edu/files/galleries/gfte-crete.pdf.

Keum, Jooseop, ed. *Together Towards Life: Mission and Evangelism in Changing Landscapes*. Geneva: WCC, 2013.

Kim, Kirsteen. "The Future of Mission Studies." *Transformation* 41 (2024) 1–9.

———. *Joining in with the Spirit. Connecting World Church and Local Mission*. London: Epworth, 2009.

———. "Mission: Integrated or Autonomous? Implications for the Study of World Christianity." In *Ecumenism and Independency in World Christianity: Historical Studies in Honour of Brian Stanley*, edited by Alexander Chow and Emma Wild-Wood, 62–80. Theology and Mission in World Christianity 15. Leiden: Brill, 2020.

Kim, Kirsteen, et al., eds. *The Oxford Handbook of Mission Studies*. Oxford: Oxford University Press, 2022.

Kim, Sinwoong. *Mission as Process: Korean Missionaries' Critical Christocentric-Trinitarian Approach to Missio Dei in their Reverse Missionary Endeavours in England*. Amsterdam: Vrije Universiteit, 2019.

Kinsler, Ross, ed. *Diversified Theological Education: Equipping All God's People*. Pasadena CA: William Carey International University Press, 2008.

Klein, Naomi. *Doppelganger: A Trip into the Mirror World*. London: Penguin, 2023.

Bibliography

———. *This Changes Everything*. London: Penguin, 2014.

———. "The Zone of Interest Is About the Danger of Ignoring Atrocities—Including in Gaza." *The Guardian*, Mar. 14, 2024. https://www.theguardian.com/commentisfree/2024/mar/14/the-zone-of-interest-auschwitz-gaza-genocide.

Kollman, Paul. "The Urgent Demands of the Present: Missiological Discernment in a Wounded World." *Mission Studies* 39 (2022) 139–62.

Kwiyani, Harvey. "Mission After George Floyd: On White Supremacy, Colonialism and World Christianity." *ANVIL* 36 (2020). https://churchmissionsociety.org/anvil/mission-after-george-floyd-on-white-supremacy-colonialism-and-world-christianity-harvey-kwiyani-anvil-vol-36-issue-3/.

Lalrinthanga, H. "Cooperation and Unity Among the Mission Churches in Mizoram." In *Transformative Rethinking: Christian Mission and Cooperation in a Multireligious Indian Society*, edited by Jamir Chongpongmeren and H. Lalrinthanga, 83–92. International Missionary Council Centenary Series. Oxford: Regnum, 2024.

Latourette, Kenneth Scott. "Ecumenical Bearings of the Missionary Movement and the International Missionary Council." In *A History of the Ecumenical Movement*, edited by Ruth Rouse and Stephen Charles Neill, 1:352–402. Geneva: WCC, 2004.

Lausanne Movement. "The Seoul Statement." https://lausanne.org/statement/the-seoul-statement.

Lawmsanga. "Theology of Mission: The Mizo Perspective." In *Witnessing to Christ in North East India*, edited by Marina Ngursangzeli and Michael Biehl, 47–58. Regnum Edinburgh Centenary Series 31. Oxford: Regnum, 2016.

Lewis, Alan. *Between Cross and Resurrection: A Theology of Holy Saturday*. Grand Rapids: Eerdmans, 2001.

"The Living Planet: Seeking a Just and Sustainable Global Community." In *Christ's Love Moves the World to Reconciliation and Unity: Report of the World Council of Churches 11th Assembly, Karlsruhe, Germany, 2022*, 175–81. Geneva: WCC, 2023.

Lubaale, Nicta. "Independents." In *Christianity in Sub-Saharan Africa*, edited by Kenneth R. Ross et al., 252–63. Edinburgh Companion to Global Christianity. Edinburgh: Edinburgh University Press, 2017.

Ma, Wonsuk, and Kenneth R. Ross, eds. *Mission Spirituality and Authentic Discipleship*. Regnum Edinburgh Centenary Series 14. Oxford: Regnum, 2013.

Macquarrie, John. "The Figure of Jesus Christ in Contemporary Christianity." In *Companion Encyclopedia of Theology*, edited by Peter Byrne and Leslie Houlden, 917–36. London: Routledge, 1995.

Mair, Peter. *Ruling the Void: The Hollowing of Western Democracy*. London: Verso, 2013.

Maluleke, Tinyiko. "Wounded Healers in the Service of the Wounded: The Case of South Africa." In *Together in the Mission of God: Jubilee Reflections on the International Missionary Council*, edited by Risto Jukko, 125–49. Geneva: WCC, 2022.

Mann, Geoff. "The Inequality Machine." *London Review of Books* 42 (2020) 25–28.

———. "Treading Thin Air." *London Review of Books* 45 (2023) 16–19.

Mateus, Odair Pedroso. "On Moltmann, Sodepax and the Ecumenical Origins of Liberation Theology." World Council of Churches, Jan. 8, 2020. https://www.oikoumene.org/news/on-moltmann-sodepax-and-the-ecumenical-origins-of-liberation-theology.

Matthey, Jacques, ed. *"Come, Holy Spirit, Heal and Reconcile!" Report of the WCC Conference on World Mission and Evangelism, Athens, Greece, May 9–16, 2005*. Geneva: WCC, 2008.

McGuire, Bill. *Hothouse Earth: An Inhabitant's Guide*. London: Icon, 2022.

Bibliography

McKibben, Bill. *Deep Economy: The Wealth of Communities and the Durable Future.* New York: Times, 2007.

Meek, James. Review of Barbara F. Walter, *How Civil Wars Start—and How to Stop Them*. *London Review of Books* 44 (2022) 3–8.

Miles, Glenn, and Ian de Villiers. "Christian NGOs and Their Role in Holistic Mission." In *Holistic Mission: God's Plan for God's People*, edited by Brian Woolnough and Wonsuk Ma, 149–59. Regnum Edinburgh Centenary Series 5. Oxford: Regnum, 2010.

Mills, Greg, et al. *Democracy Works: Rewiring Politics to Africa's Advantage.* Johannesburg: Picador Africa, 2019.

Mission and Decolonization. International Review of Mission 112.2 (2023).

"Mission and Evangelism. An Evangelical Affirmation." In *"You are the Light of the World": Statements on Mission by the World Council of Churches, 1980–2005*, 1–38. Geneva: WCC, 2005.

"Mission and Evangelism in Unity Today." In *"You are the Light of the World": Statements on Mission by the World Council of Churches, 1980–2005*, 62–89. Geneva: WCC, 2005.

"Missional Formation: Transforming the World. Equipping the Disciples." In *Conference on World Mission and Evangelism, 2018: Complete Digital Edition of the Arusha Report*, edited by Risto Jukko, 147–72. Geneva: WCC, 2019.

Mizoram Presbyterian Church. "Synod Mission Board (SMB)." https://www.mizoramsynod.org/page/1787.

Moltmann, Jürgen. "Christianity: A Religion of Joy." In *Joy and Human Flourishing*, edited by Miroslav Volf and Justin E. Crisp, 1–15. Philadelphia: Fortress, 2015.

———. *Theology of Hope: On the Ground and the Implications for a Christian Eschatology.* London: SCM, 2002.

Monbiot, George. "Here's a Question COP28 Won't Address: Why Are Billionaires Blocking Action to Save the Planet?" *The Guardian*, Nov. 29, 2023. https://www.theguardian.com/commentisfree/2023/nov/29/cop28-billionaires-blocking-action-save-planet-protest.

———. *Out of the Wreckage: A New Politics for an Age of Crisis.* London: Verso, 2017.

———. "With Our Food Systems on the Verge of Collapse, It's the Plutocrats v Life on Earth." *The Guardian*, July 15, 2023. https://www.theguardian.com/commentisfree/2023/jul/15/food-systems-collapse-plutocrats-life-on-earth-climate-breakdown.

Morsello, Barbara, et al. "'This Is the Real Face of Covid-19!': How Refused Knowledge Communities Entered the Pandemic Arena." In *Manufacturing Refused Knowledge in the Age of Epistemic Pluralism: Discourses, Imaginaries, and Practices on the Border of Science*, edited by Frederico Neresini et al., 195–223. Singapore: Springer Nature Singapore, 2024.

Mount, Ferdinand. "Après Brexit." *London Review of Books* 42 (2020) 7–10.

Mshana, Rogate R. "Human Mind and Heart and Artificial Intelligence: An African Perspective." In *Humanity and Spirituality in Face of the Fourth Industrial Revolution*, edited by Seong-Won Park, 36–38. Gyeongsan: Life in Beauty, 2017.

Nagel, Alexander-Kenneth. "Die Gegenwart der Endzeit. Denkmodelle und Forschungsperspektiven." In *Endzeit ohne Ende? Gegenwelten, Unzeiten, Nichtorte*. Berliner Theologische Zeitschrift 35 (2018) 169–88.

The New Delhi Report. The Third Assembly of the World Council of Churches 1961. London: SCM, 1962.

Bibliography

Newbigin, Lesslie. "Cross-Currents in Ecumenical and Evangelical Understandings of Mission." *International Bulletin of Missionary Research* 6 (1982) 146–51.

———. *One Body One Gospel One World: The Christian Mission Today*. London: International Missionary Council, 1958.

———. *The Open Secret: Sketches for a Missionary Theology*. Grand Rapids: Eerdmans, 1978.

Nguyên, Vănthanh. "Mission and Biblical Studies: Convergences, Challenges, and Prospects." In *The Oxford Handbook of Mission Studies*, edited by Kirsteen Kim et al., 77–94. Oxford: Oxford University Press, 2022.

Niranjan, Ajit. "2023 on Track to be the Hottest Year on Record, Say Scientists." *The Guardian*, Nov. 8, 2023. https://www.theguardian.com/environment/2023/nov/08/2023-on-track-to-be-the-hottest-year-on-record-say-scientists.

Njehu, Njoki. "Foreword." In *Climate Equality: A Planet for the 99%*, by Oxfam, viii. Oxford: Oxfam International, November 2023.

Noort, Gerrit. "'So What?'—Dutch Responses to the New Mission Statement." *International Review of Mission* 102 (2013) 191–98.

Noort, Gerrit, et al., eds. *Sharing Good News: Handbook on Evangelism in Europe*. Geneva: WCC, 2017.

Nordin, Magdalena, and Jonas Otterbeck. *Migration and Religion*. IMISCOE Short Reader. Cham: Springer Nature, 2023.

Olofinjana, Israel Oluwole, ed. *World Christianity in Western Europe: Diasporic Identity, Narratives and Missiology*. Regnum Studies in Mission. Oxford: Regnum, 2020.

Ott, Bernhard. *Beyond Fragmentation: Integrating Mission and Theological Education; A Critical Assessment of Some Recent Developments in Evangelical Theological Education*. Regnum Studies in Mission. Oxford: Regnum, 2011.

Oxfam. *Are G20 Countries Doing Their Fair Share of Global Climate Mitigation?* Oxfam Discussion Paper, 2023.

———. *Climate Equality: A Planet for the 99%*. Oxford: Oxfam International, November 2023.

Padel, Felix. "In the Name of Sustainable Development: Genocide Masked as 'Tribal Development.'" In *First Citizens: Studies on Adivasis, Tribals, and Indigenous Peoples in India*, edited by Meena Radhakrishna, 159–77. Oxford India Studies in Contemporary Society. New Delhi: Oxford University Press, 2016.

Pandemic and Pedagogy: Ecumenical Consultation on Theological Education. https://www.oikoumene.org/sites/default/files/2023-06/Pedagogy-and-Pandemic-Communique%CC%81.pdf.

"Panel Interview with Kwabena Asamoah-Gyadu, Kirsteen Kim, and Youhanon Mar Demetrios." In *Conference on World Mission and Evangelism, 2018*. Complete Digital Edition of the Arusha Report, edited by Risto Jukko, 151–57. Geneva: WCC, 2019.

Pannenberg, Wolfhart. *What Is Man? Contemporary Anthropology in Theological Perspective*. Philadelphia: Fortress, 1970.

Park, Seong-Won, ed. *Humanity and Spirituality in Face of the Fourth Industrial Revolution*. Gyeongsan: Life in Beauty, 2017.

The Participation of Women in the Ordained Ministry and Leadership in LWF Member Churches. Geneva: Lutheran World Federation, 2016. https://lutheranworld.org/sites/default/files/dtpw-wicas_women_ordination.pdf.

BIBLIOGRAPHY

Phan, Peter C. "Developments of the Doctrine of the Trinity." In *The Cambridge Companion to The Trinity*, edited by Peter C. Phan, 3–12. Cambridge: Cambridge University Press, 2011.

Phiri, Isabel, and Dietrich Werner, eds. *African Handbook on Theological Education*. Oxford: Regnum, 2013.

Piketty, Thomas. *Capital in the Twenty-First Century*. Boston: Harvard University Press, 2014.

The Preparation of Missionaries. Report of Commission V. World Missionary Conference, 1910. Edinburgh, London: Oliphant, Anderson & Ferrier, n.d.

Rahner, Karl. *The Trinity*. New York: The Crossroad, 2005.

Reinbold, Wolfgang. "Gehet hin und machet zu Jüngern alle Völker!? Zur Übersetzung und Interpretation von Mt 28, 19f." *Zeitschrift für Theologie und Kirche* 109 (2012) 176–205.

Renewal and Advance. Christian Witness in a Revolutionary World. Edited by C. W. Ransom. London: Edinburgh House, 1948.

Rivera-Pagán, Luis N. *God, in Your Grace . . . Official Report of the Ninth Assembly of the World Council of Churches*. Geneva: WCC, 2007.

Robert, Dana L. *Christian Mission. How Christianity became a World Religion*. Chichester, UK: Wiley-Blackwell, 2009.

———. "Historical Trends in Missions and Earth Care." *International Bulletin of Missionary Research* 35 (2011) 123–28.

Robert, Dana L., et al., eds. *Creative Collaborations: Case Studies of North American Missional Practices*. International Missionary Council Centenary Series. Oxford: Regnum, 2023.

Rosin, Hans H. *Missio Dei: An Examination of the Origin, Contents and Function of the Term in Protestant Missiological Discussion*. Leiden: Inter-University Institute for Missiological and Ecumenical Research, 1972.

Ross, Kenneth R. "The Arusha Call: Signal of Missiological Convergence?" *International Review of Mission* 107 (2018) 443–57.

———. "Contemporary Ecumenical Missiology and the Renewal of Christian Theology." *Transformation* 40:3 (2023) 181–91.

———. *Mission Rediscovered: Transforming Disciples; A Commentary on the Arusha Call to Discipleship*. Geneva: Globethics, 2020.

Ross, Kenneth R., et al., eds. *Christianity in Sub-Saharan Africa*. Edinburgh Companions to Global Christianity. Edinburgh: Edinburgh University Press, 2017.

———. *Ecumenical Missiology: Changing Landscapes and New Conceptions of Mission*. Geneva: WCC, 2016.

Rouse, Ruth, and Stephen Charles Neill, eds. *A History of the Ecumenical Movement*. Vol. 1: *1517–1948*. 3rd ed. Geneva: WCC, 2004.

Salama, Ibrahim, and Michael Wiener. "Religion and Human Rights: From Conversion to Convergence." In *Strengthening Christian Perspectives on Human Dignity and Human Rights: Perspectives from an International Consultation Process*, edited by Peter Prove et al., 129–36. Geneva: WCC & Globethics.net, 2022.

The São Paulo Statement: International Financial Transformation for the Economy of Life. Geneva: WCC, WCRC, Council for World Mission, 2012. https://www.oikoumene.org/resources/documents/sao-paulo-statement-international-financial-transformation-for-the-economy-of-life.

Bibliography

Schreiter, Robert J. *The Ministry of Reconciliation: Spirituality and Strategies.* Maryknoll, NY: Orbis, 1998.

———. *The New Catholicity: Theology Between the Global and the Local.* Faith and Cultures Series. Maryknoll, NY: Orbis, 1997.

Senturias, Erlinda N., and Theodore A. Gill Jr., eds. *Encountering the God of Life: Report of the 10th Assembly of the World Council of Churches.* Geneva: WCC, 2014.

Singh, David Emmanuel, and Bernard C. Farr, eds. *Christianity and Education. Shaping Christian Thinking in Context.* Regnum Studies in Global Christianity. Oxford: Regnum, 2011.

Snodderly, Beth, and A. Scott Moreau, eds. *Evangelical and Frontier Mission: Perspectives on the Global Progress of the Gospel.* Regnum Edinburgh 2010 Series. Oxford: Regnum, 2011.

Solnit, Rebecca. *Hope in the Dark: Untold Histories, Wild Possibilities.* Edinburgh: Canongate, 2015.

Sonea, Cristian, et al., eds. *The Heritage of Mission Today: Historical and Intercultural Perspectives.* International Missionary Council Centenary Series. Oxford: Regnum, 2024.

Souza, Luis Wesley de. "Spirituality." In *Together in the Mission of God: Jubilee Reflections on the International Missionary Council,* edited by Risto Jukko, 261–93. Oxford: Regnum, 2022.

Stanley, Brian. "Where Have Our Mission Structures Come From?" *Transformation* 20 (2003) 39–46.

Stevenson, Tom. "Empires in Disguise." *London Review of Books* 45 (2023) 11–12.

Stransky, Thomas F. "The World Congress of Evangelism, Berlin." *The Secretariat for Promoting Christian Unity Information Service* (1967) 15–16.

Stroope, Michael W. *Transcending Mission: The Eclipse of a Modern Tradition.* Downers Grove, IL: InterVarsity, 2017.

Sung, Jung Mo. *Desire, Market and Religion.* London: SCM, 2007.

Thomas, Norman E. *Missions and Unity: Lessons from History, 1792–2010.* Eugene, OR: Cascade, 2010.

Thunberg, Greta. "Foreword." In *Climate Equality: A Planet for the 99%,* by Oxfam, vi–vii. Oxford: Oxfam International, 2023.

Truman, Harry S. "Inaugural Address, January 20, 1949." https://www.trumanlibrary.gov/library/public-papers/19/inaugural-address.

United Nations. "Transforming Our World: The 2030 Agenda for Sustainable Development." https://sdgs.un.org/2030agenda.

UNHCR. "About UNHCR." https://www.unhcr.org/about-unhcr.

———. "Who We Protect: Internally Displaced People." https://www.unhcr.org/about-unhcr/who-we-protect/internally-displaced-people

———. "Who We Protect: Refugees." https://www.unhcr.org/refugees.

van Den Heuvel, Steven, ed. *Historical and Multidisciplinary Perspectives on Hope.* Springer: Cham, 2020.

van Saane, Wilbert, and John Holdsworth, eds. *Christian Mission in the Middle East. Ecumenical Perspectives.* International Missionary Council Centenary Series. Oxford: Regnum, 2024.

Vassiliadis, Petros, ed. *Orthodox Perspectives on Mission.* Oxford: Regnum, 2013.

BIBLIOGRAPHY

Visser 't Hooft, Willem Adolph, ed. *The First Assembly of the World Council of Churches Held at Amsterdam, August 22nd to September 4th, 1948.* Man's Disorder and God's Design 5. London: SCM, 1949.

———. "The Word 'Ecumenical'—Its History and Use." In *A History of the Ecumenical Movement*, edited by Ruth Rouse and Stephen Charles Neill, 1:735–40. Geneva: WCC, 2004.

Volf, Miroslav, and Justin Crisp, eds. *Joy and Human Flourishing. Essays on Theology, Culture, and the Good Life.* Philadelphia: Fortress, 2015.

Walls, Andrew F. *The Cross-Cultural Process in Christian History.* Maryknoll, NY: Orbis, 2002.

Warneck, Gustav. *Evangelische Missionslehre. Ein missionstheologischer Versuch. 1. Abteilung: Die Begründung der Sendung.* 2nd ed. Gotha: Friedrich Andreas Perthes, 1897.

Werner, Dietrich. *Training to Be Ministers in Asia: Contextualizing Theological Education in Multi-Faith Contexts.* PTCA Series No 3. Tainan: PTCA, 2012.

Werner, Dietrich, et al., eds. *Handbook of Theological Education in World Christianity: Theological Perspectives, Ecumenical Trends, Regional Surveys.* Oxford: Regnum, 2010.

White, Lynn, Jr. "The Historical Roots of our Ecologic Crisis." *Science* 155 (1967) 1203–7.

Wilson, Frederick R., ed. *The San Antonio Report. Your Will Be Done. Mission in Christ's Way.* Geneva: WCC, 1990.

Winter, Ralph D. "Will Uppsala Betray the Two Billion?" *Church Growth Bulletin* 4 (1968) 1–6.

Wood, David. *Poet, Priest and Prophet: Bishop John V. Taylor.* London: CTBI, 2002.

Woodberry, Robert D. "The Missionary Roots of Liberal Democracy." *American Political Science Review* 106 (2012) 244–74.

World Alliance of Reformed Churches. *Accra Confession: Covenanting for Justice in the Economy and the Earth.* Geneva: WARC, 2004.

World Report on the Future of Theological Education in the 21st Century: Theological Education in World Christianity. Joint Information Service of ETE/WCC & WOCATI, Nov. 2009.

Yong, Amos. "Primed for the Spirit: Creation, Redemption and the *Missio Spiritus*." *International Review of Mission* 100 (2011) 355–66.

"You Are the Light of the World": Statements on Mission by the World Council of Churches 1980–2005. Geneva: WCC, 2005.

Zurlo, Gina. *From Nairobi to the World: David B. Barrett and the Re-imagining of World Christianity.* Theology and Mission in World Christianity 26. Leiden: Brill, 2023.

Zurlo, Gina, et al. "World Christianity and Mission 2021: Questions about the Future." *International Bulletin of Mission Research* 45 (2021) 15–25.